SECRETS
FROM
THE BOOK
FOR THE
PEOPLE
OF THE
VALLEY

Secrets from THE BOOK

J. STEPHEN

WITH TEXT

'or the people of the valley

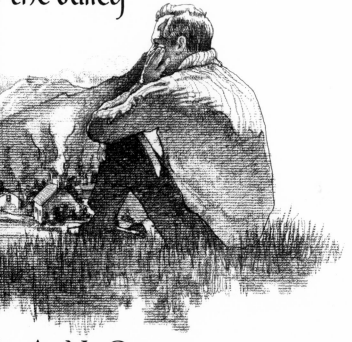

LANG

FROM THE BOOK

Tyndale House Publishers, Inc.   Wheaton, Illinois

Cover and interior illustrations by
Ron DiCianni

Scripture verses are from *The Book*,
a special edition of *The Living Bible*,
published by
Tyndale House Publishers, Inc.

The Living Bible
© owned by assignment
by Illinois Regional Bank N.A.
(as trustee).
All rights reserved.

Library of Congress Catalog Card Number 89-50923
ISBN 0-8423-5844-7
Copyright © 1989 by J. Stephen Lang
All rights reserved
Printed in the United States of America

1 2 3 4 5 6 7 8 94 93 92 91 90 89

TO

L. T. Wolcott

TEACHER

AUTHOR

FRIEND

Truth is so obscure
in these times,
and falsehood so established,
that, unless we love the truth,
we cannot know it.

BLAISE PASCAL

Then began I with sad
and careful heart
to search into the Word of God,
if I could in any place
find a word of promise,
or any encouraging sentence,
by which I might take relief.

JOHN BUNYAN

CONTENTS

THE PEOPLE
OF THE
VALLEY

*T*HE People of the Valley
had days of sunshine, days of rain. Like most people
everywhere, they laughed, they cried, they brought
children into the world, they buried the dead, they
sang, they danced, they built, they tore down.

Martin was one of the People of the Valley. He had
lived in the Valley all his days, as had his father and
mother and his grandfathers and grandmothers. He
had been taught that there would be joyful days and
sad days, and he learned that this was indeed so. He
had seen his youth pass, and he had watched his parents grow old. He had seen his own children growing
up before his eyes, and he knew he was doing what
people do everywhere.

Knowing this pleased Martin. One cool day he was
seated on a hillside, overlooking the houses in the
Valley. He looked at his own home, with its smoke
curling skyward. He was pleased that he had built a
cozy place for his wife and his children and, someday,
for his grandchildren. He reflected on his joyful days
and his sorrowful days and wondered if he had any
cause to be bitter. He could think of none, though
somehow he felt restless.

Then he thought of his old grandfather, who had

died many years ago. Before his death the old man had drawn the young Martin to his side and told him, "Search for the Truth, Martin. Everything else is decoration. Everything else in this life is passing, failing, fading away. Search for the Truth, whatever else you do in this life."

And young Martin had promised himself to do this. But he was young, and since no one reminded him of his promise to himself, he forgot the promise.

Now Martin was seated on a hillside, wondering if he had the time or the vigor to keep the promise to himself, wondering if it was worth the trouble after all. But something told him that it was worth the trouble.

Martin was looking down upon the houses of the Valley. But something made him turn and look over his shoulder. Suddenly he noticed a traveler he did not know climbing up the back side of the hill. The Unknown Traveler carried a walking stick, and in his face he looked weary but determined. Halfway up the hillside he stopped and took a drink from the canteen at his side. Then he paused for a moment, looked carefully at Martin, and proceeded up the hill.

Martin watched the Unknown Traveler. *Perhaps,* Martin thought, *this is one of the buyers who was to call on me today.* But Martin was not in the mood to talk to people about buying and selling. He was thinking about his promise made years ago.

"A lovely day, yes?" said the Unknown Traveler as he stood before Martin. "Cool, but pleasant all in all, wouldn't you say?"

"Pleasant, yes," Martin replied, sizing up the Traveler who stood in front of him. "I don't believe I know you. Are you one of the buyers?"

The Unknown Traveler removed his brown felt

hat—its style was not familiar to Martin—dusted it off, and sat down beside Martin. "No, I am no buyer, sir. Just traveling through, you might say. Who might I have the honor of speaking to?"

"My name is Martin. I live here in this Valley. And who are you?"

The Traveler's eyes surveyed the Valley, and Martin could see he did not intend to answer the question.

"You live in a beautiful place, sir," the Traveler said. "You are grateful, I think, to live in a place not much removed from heaven, yes?"

"Not far from heaven? No, indeed, not like heaven. People die here, people hurt one another, children grieve their parents, parents grieve their children. I have fallen asleep at the end of a day and said to myself, 'Pity that this glorious day has an ending.' Yet on some nights I have fallen asleep, glad to escape whatever the day's sorrows had been. Pain and pleasure, blessing and burden, day after day after day. Good and ill, all mingled together—so, not so much like heaven."

The Unknown Traveler shifted so as to face Martin better. He had intense brown eyes, and he looked directly at Martin as he spoke.

"Were you brought into this world and told you would have only bright days and peaceful nights?"

"No, no one ever told me such a thing. I was prepared for the evil days, though never too pleased when they came. But no one bothered to tell me what it all meant. No one explained why it was worth it, after all was said and done, to live through the good days and the bad days. No one told me I would ever pause as I do today and wonder if I had pursued the right things, loved the right things, looked at this world through the proper lens."

The Unknown Traveler leaned toward Martin as if he were going to tell a great secret. Martin in turn leaned toward him, waiting to hear something he had not heard before.

"Listen," said the Traveler. "You believe you alone are a thinker among the People of the Valley. You think you are the only one wondering about these things. How wrong you are, Martin. The promise you made to yourself years ago was a promise that many others made. But along the way they lost sight of that, and they forgot about the Truth. Now they wonder if it is too late to search, and whether it is worth their while."

Martin did not pause to puzzle over how the Unknown Traveler knew of the promise he had made many years ago. He knew that what the Traveler had said was true, so he saw no point in wondering why or how he knew.

"I am no longer young," Martin said. "I have much to keep me busy. My days are full. Promises made in youth cannot always be kept. Still—"

"Still, it is important to you. It is more important than any thought that ever was kindled in your head." The Traveler stood, picked up his walking stick, and put on his hat. "Martin, today the Maker of this Valley wants so much for you to remember your promise. He wants everyone to search for the Truth. In fact, he has laid it at your feet, yet you have forgotten it was there." At this the Traveler turned and began striding down the hill.

"Wait!" Martin shouted as he saw the Traveler moving quickly down the hill. He ran to catch up with him and caught him by the sleeve.

The Traveler turned and gazed into his eyes again. Martin looked like a begging child as he said, "You seem so wise. I wish to talk with you. I would like to keep the promise that I made years ago. You could teach me many things."

"Ah, Martin, no. I have nothing to tell you that you cannot find in The Book."

Martin paused and chewed on his lip for a moment. "The Book?"

"Yes, Martin—think, think back, think long thoughts. You must recall it."

"I remember The Book. I heard my grandparents speak of it years ago. We have it in the Valley somewhere. It's—it's—yes, I remember. It's in a vault underneath the town square."

"Find The Book, Martin. If you want to keep your promise, find The Book. If you seek the Truth, you must begin your search by finding The Book."

"Is The Book—it is the Truth, then?" Martin was pleased that he could find the key to the truth so quickly, but he distrusted anything that seemed too easy.

"It is the *key* to the Truth. It points to the Truth, and it is rooted in the Truth. The Truth is . . ."

"Yes, yes, tell me. Don't leave me wondering." Martin looked like a small boy, even though his hair was already flecked with gray and his forehead had started to furrow.

"The Truth is not words or thoughts you can define or put a leash on. The Truth is the Creator himself. You meet with the Truth when you meet with him."

"But we can't see the Creator," Martin said anxiously. His eyes were wide with wonder. "I've never heard him speak. I don't know where to find him."

"He reigns."

"That much I believe, yes," Martin said anxiously. "But he does not speak as I now speak with you. So how can I find the Truth, then? If I were to hear his voice . . ."

The Unknown Traveler looked with kindness on Martin. "Listen, Martin. I will teach you something from The Book. What I will tell you is about the Creator, the Truth."

The Traveler paused and looked around the Valley, at its homes and streets. Then he turned again to Martin and spoke these words:

Long ago God spoke in many different ways to our fathers through the prophets in visions, dreams, and even face to face, telling them little by little about his plans.

But now in these days he has spoken to us through his Son to whom he has given everything, and through whom he made the world and everything there is. God's Son shines out with God's glory, and all that God's Son is and does marks him as God.

"Do you understand that, Martin?"

"You are telling me—The Book is telling me— that the Creator has communicated with us through prophets, but that later he spoke through a Son. But what does that Son have to do with The Book?"

"All you know about the Son is to be found in The Book, Martin. If you look for the Truth, look for God. If you look for God, look for the Son. If you look for the Son, open The Book."

The Traveler again started down the hill. Again Martin ran after him. "Wait! I am afraid—afraid that I cannot read The Book even if I find it."

The Traveler stopped and gazed at Martin. "The Book was written for all time, for every man and woman who ever will live. You will understand it. But because you are afraid, I will go with you into the Valley and help you, for now. Come with me, for we haven't much time."

Martin tugged on the sleeve of the Traveler. "Tell me who you are, please."

"That does not matter. You never promised to look for me. You were looking for the Truth. Come with me; let us together find The Book."

FINDING
THE BOOK

*T*HE People of the Valley were not at all surprised by strangers, but somehow the Unknown Traveler who accompanied Martin began to draw their attention. Martin and his new companion walked with a determination of two men on a mission. And though no one in the Valley had ever seen the Traveler, he seemed familiar with every turn in the road. It was as though he, not Martin, was leading the way.

The two arrived at the square, where Martin noticed many more people than usual. As he looked about him, he realized that everyone in the Valley was there. Such a thing never happened, not even for the Valley's festivals. But as Martin glanced around, he could not think of a soul he knew who was not there. He was puzzled, and the Traveler puzzled him as well. But his confusion was small compared to his remembrance of his commitment to the Truth.

"Martin," the Traveler said, looking at the rustling poplar leaves as if he knew them well, "you said you could recall where The Book is."

"There is a vault under the gazebo here at the center of the square. See, there are the steps leading down to it." The Traveler could see that the door at the bottom of the steps had not been moved in many a year. Rust was caked about the hinges, and the spiders had done their part to shroud the entrance.

"My grandfather talked about playing in the vault when he was a boy. He said it was a place where the Valley's archives were stored. I suppose the children had enough respect for the Valley's traditions that they could play there without disturbing anything. But no one has been down there for as long as I can remember. Everything down there may have crumbled into dust by now."

"And The Book is down there?"

Martin hesitated, wondering if he had spoken rashly earlier. He had no proof that The Book was anywhere to be found. He had only an old man's memory to go on. Yet something told him The Book was indeed still there.

"I hope it is there. But I don't know who has the key to the vault. And the lock in the door may be too rusty to turn." While he was still speaking the Traveler had descended the steps. He brushed aside the dusty webs and touched the latch on the door. It moved slightly. Then the hinges squealed painfully, and the noise made Martin wince. The Traveler stepped inside the ancient room, and Martin followed him.

Even under decades of dust the archives were still intact. From what Martin could tell the books and papers were mostly family histories. Some appeared to be gatherings of laws, and some appeared to be poetry. In one corner of the room was a doll, left long ago by a child who must have seen the place of tradition as a place for play.

The Traveler's eyes surveyed the shelves and tables. Books there were, yet his face showed that his gaze had not yet settled on The Book they had come for. Martin strained his mind, trying to recall whether his grandfather had described The Book to him.

"It was large, I think, and heavy. Its binding was leather, etched with gold. My grandfather said it was beautiful."

"It is indeed," the Traveler said. He reached under a heap of papers underneath a table. When he stood up he was holding a volume with several layers of dust. It appeared that some of the dust was etched forever into the binding. But when the Traveler blew on the surface, it fell away as if it had never belonged there.

The Traveler laid down his walking stick and opened The Book at its center. Then he began to read.

Nothing is worthwhile; everything is futile. Everything is unutterably weary and tiresome.

As I looked at everything I had tried, it was all so useless, a chasing of the wind, and there was nothing really worthwhile anywhere.

He lifted his eyes from the page and fixed them on Martin's face. "This is an old book, Martin. We are standing here in the midst of oldness. These things here have nothing to say to you, perhaps." And he began to shut The Book. But Martin stopped him.

"No, no, please. Those words—they are not mine, but the heart underneath them is mine. I am a restless man, a wondering man, a man so perplexed by the here and the now that the past does not seem much stranger than the present. Whoever penned those words knew me, or someone like me." Then Martin felt himself the fool for baring his vague anxiety to a stranger. But this passed, and he asked the Traveler, "Is there more in The Book than the sad declarations of the anxious?"

"Indeed, there is more," the Traveler said, and he reopened The Book and read these words:

Can you not hear the voice of wisdom? She is standing at the city gates and at every fork in the road, and at the door of every house. Listen to what she says: "Listen!" she calls. "How foolish and naive you are! Let me give you understanding. My instruction is far more valuable than silver or gold.

"The Lord formed me in the beginning, before he created anything else. From ages past, I am. I existed before the earth began. I lived before the oceans were created, before the springs bubbled forth their waters onto the earth; before the mountains and the hills were made. Yes, I was born before God made the earth and fields, and the first handfuls of soil.

"Listen to my counsel—oh, don't refuse it—and be wise. Happy is the man who is so anxious to be with me that he watches for me daily at my gates, or waits for me outside my home! For whoever finds me finds life and wins approval from the Lord. The one who misses me has injured himself irreparably. Those who refuse me show that they love death."

The Unknown Traveler paused for a moment, and Martin's eyes scanned the page. The words were in his language, yet it seemed as if a mist hung over them, obscuring them. Martin could not tell if the mist was on The Book or in his own eyes. But the Traveler had no trouble reading.

The reverence and fear of God are basic to all wisdom. Knowing God results in every other kind of understanding.

"This," the Traveler said, "is The Book of God, God who loves the despondent and the perplexed. This is God's Book for Martin, and for all seeking the Truth. And you are not the only one, Martin." Then he shut The Book, but Martin was sure he would open it again.

"Come, Martin. It is late in the year. These autumn days are short. Your neighbors are all gathered in the square, and they must hear these words this day." He took up his walking stick and moved toward the steps.

"Wait," Martin said. "They may not listen. This is only an ancient bundle of leather and paper to them. What could the words mean?"

"I cannot promise you that they will listen. I cannot promise you that you will listen further. The Book is not a weapon of coercion. It is The Book of God, and he does not bludgeon people with the Truth. Some will listen, as you did just now. And some will not. And some who listen will not understand, or want to. This is nothing new or strange. Almighty God breathed his life into creatures capable of loving him—or running away. The God of The Book is a risking God."

When Martin heard this, his own doubts were dispelled. He did not know why. He was not sure his neighbors would be so quick to accept The Book. Yet he hoped they would.

The Traveler walked up the steps and into the gazebo. No one had called the People of the Valley together, yet all were there, as if they expected music and dancing in the square. Yet festivity was not in the cool air. Some were there carrying curiosity in their heads, and others carried a readiness to scorn, for there were those who believed that the nagging questions in this life had no real answers. But some were there carrying hope and anticipation. And some were there carrying burdens they wished to be rid of.

Martin stepped into the gazebo, believing he would need to introduce the Unknown Traveler to

23

the People of the Valley. But the Traveler stood there as if the whole picture had been painted long before. And Martin joined his neighbors in the square.

"This is The Book of God, God the Father, God who made everything. There is nothing in the world like God. He made this world and reigned over it and treasured it, and he still does so. And long ago he entered it as a man himself. So the lofty One has been where you are—walking on the earth, sweating on humid days, wincing when a splinter pierced his palm, crying over a departed friend, living, feasting, fasting, sorrowing, bleeding, dying."

A few of the older ones nodded, for they could remember hearing of the Son of God who walked the earth. They could remember hearing of this Father who would pour out both discipline and tenderness. Some could even remember hearing of The Book, though this was the first time they had ever seen it.

"The Book is here to disturb you, and to comfort you, and to bring you joy. It is to remind you who God is, and who you are."

As the clouds of October passed their shadows over the Valley's rooftops, the Traveler read these words uttered by the Son of God:

My purpose is to give life in all its fullness.

If anyone is thirsty, let him come to me and drink. For rivers of living water shall flow from the inmost being of anyone who believes in me.

You will know the truth, and the truth will set you free.

Many of the People of the Valley were thirsty, and many wanted the truth. And all wanted life in its fullness. So the gates of most hearts there were left ajar.

24

PAIN
AND
SORROW

SEBASTIAN and Julia, who had known much suffering, stood by as they listened to the words from The Book. Sebastian's tired old eyes looked up at the cool gray autumn sky and he wondered if it might rain. Julia looked at her husband and knew he had seen so much pain in life and had come to think there was no hope for it. Though she was a shy and timid woman by nature, she stepped forward and, trembling a little, spoke to the Unknown Traveler.

"Sir, you tell us about the Creator who made this world and everything in it. I believe in that Creator, and so does my poor husband here. But we have known so much hurt. Our children are all dead. We have lost almost everything we once owned. So many times we have suffered in sickness. Tell us, if there is anything good to tell, about sorrow."

The Unknown Traveler looked for a long time into the tired old eyes of Julia. A tiny tear rolled down his cheek, but then he smiled, as if he knew he could give her what she had asked for. Then he lifted up The Book and began to speak.

The Lord is close to those whose hearts are breaking.
The good man does not escape all troubles—he has them too. But the Lord helps him in each and every one.

25

He heals the brokenhearted, binding up their wounds.

We are pressed on every side by troubles, but not crushed and broken. We are perplexed because we do not know why things happen as they do, but we do not give up and quit. We are hunted down, but God never abandons us. We get knocked down, but we get up again and keep going.

That is why we never give up. These troubles and sufferings of ours are, after all, quite small and will not last very long.

Yet this short time of distress will result in God's richest blessing upon us forever and ever!

So we do not look at what we can see right now, the troubles all around us, but we look forward to the joys in heaven which we have not yet seen.

The troubles will soon be over, but the joys to come will last forever.

No matter what happens, always be thankful, for this is God's will for you.

Martin was listening closely. He remembered a cold night many years ago when the home of Sebastian and Julia burned to the foundations. Looking at Sebastian's face now, he could recall the shadows cast by the leaping flames on the man's bewildered countenance. And the shrieking of Julia still echoed inside him. No one in the Valley would ever forget her frenzy over her daughter's death in the fire. Then the Traveler began to read again.

The steps of good men are directed by the Lord. He delights in each step they take. If they fall it is not fatal, for the Lord holds them with his hand.

He will never abandon his people. They will be kept safe forever.

The Lord says, "I know the plans I have for you. They are plans for good and not for evil, to give you a fu-

ture and a hope. When you pray, I will listen. You will find me when you seek me, if you look for me in earnest."

The Unknown Traveler looked around at the People of the Valley and knew that many of them had known much heartache. In some faces were marks of weariness and woe, in some only bitterness. And in some was the bland lukewarmness of resignation. He pitied these most, for they bore the twin burden of wearisome yesterdays and new days that would only reprise the old. Again he lifted up The Book and began to speak.

"Listen, people, to what a man of sorrow said about his God."

I waited patiently for God to help me; then he listened and heard my cry.

He lifted me out of the pit of despair, out from the bog and the mire, and set my feet on a hard, firm path and steadied me as I walked along.

He has given me a new song to sing, of praises to our God. Now many will hear of the glorious things he did for me, and stand in awe before the Lord, and put their trust in him.

"Now listen to the words of another man who suffered much."

You have let me sink down in desperate problems. You have seen me tossing and turning through the night. You have collected my tears and preserved them in your bottle! You have recorded every one in your book.

But you will bring me back to life again, up from the depths of the earth. You will give me greater honor than before, and turn again and comfort me.

I am trusting God—oh, praise his promises!

27

I am not afraid of anything mere man can do to me!
This one thing I know: God is for me!

Sebastian and Julia smiled a little, glad to know
that the God who gave The Book to them cared for
those who were hurting. The Unknown Traveler began to speak again, for he wanted them to know that
the Son of God, God in the flesh, was filled with
compassion for the burdened ones.

Jesus said, "Come to me and I will give you rest—all of
you who work so hard beneath a heavy yoke.
   "Wear my yoke—for it fits perfectly—and let me
teach you; for I am gentle and humble, and you shall find
rest for your souls; for I give you only light burdens."

Then the Unknown Traveler paused and said, "Do
you hesitate to believe this? Listen to one who remembered the good days in the midst of bad days."

I know how to live on almost nothing or with everything.
   I have learned the secret of contentment in every situ-
ation, whether it be a full stomach or hunger, plenty or
want, for I can do everything God asks me to with the
help of Christ who gives me the strength and power.
   We know that all that happens to us is working for our
good if we love God and are fitting into his plans.
   If God is on our side, who can ever be against us?

The Traveler paused and spoke to them, his words
settling upon them like the sweet and familiar breath
of an old companion, filled with compassion, yet
bent on telling the truth.

"You were placed in this beautiful theatre to act out
your part as stewards of the earth and worshipers of
God. And your great failing, the one that century

after century raises up walls between the Loving One and his creatures, is the yearning to worship someone else, something else, anything else but the One who merits worship. And some worship their past and their pain, paying hourly homage to it, kneeling before it, offering up their fractured hearts on it, singing hymns to their hurts. Their pain becomes a temple 'round itself, and they become the devotees of anguish. They forget that some of the sweetest anthems ever sung have poured out of those whose hearts were spent. They forget that joy comes, sometimes slowly, but eventually, inevitably, for those who love Almighty God more than their all-consuming afflictions." When old Sebastian heard these words, he knew the Traveler was one who could speak healing words. Then the Traveler began to read again, words of comfort that had fountained out of one who loved God more than his woes.

I am always thinking of the Lord; and because he is so
*   near, I never need to stumble or to fall.*
Heart, body, and soul are filled with joy.
I will praise the Lord no matter what happens.
I will constantly speak of his glories and grace.
Let all who are discouraged take heart.

The Traveler stopped reading and slowly closed The Book. But Martin and some of the others looked at him with the wide eyes of a hungry child who has just had a morsel of warm bread dropped into his quivering palm. Martin, like all the other People of the Valley, was capable of selfishness, yet sympathy sometimes wrapped itself about him, as if begging for him to look outward at another creature's anguish. And he had lived too long in this Valley not to have hurt along with his neighbors. So like a cool hand

upon the fevered brow, the Traveler soothingly
pressed these words upon them:

*The Lord is my light and my salvation; he protects me
from danger—whom shall I fear?*

*When evil men come to destroy me, they will stumble
and fall! Yes, though a mighty army marches against me,
my heart shall know no fear! I am confident that God
will save me. I cried to him and he answered me! He
freed me from all my fears.*

*I bless the holy name of God with all my heart. Yes, I
will bless the Lord and not forget the glorious things he
does for me. He surrounds me with loving-kindness and
tender mercies. He fills my life with good things! My
youth is renewed like the eagle's!*

*He is like a father to us, tender and sympathetic to
those who reverence him.*

A woman in the square winced as she heard these
words about the loving Father, for her own father had
mingled embraces with bruises. The same hands that
stroked the child's face blackened it, and the memo-
ries crouched inside her like a sullen beast. The Traveler saw from her posture and her expression that she
wanted not only healing but a father. "Listen," the
Traveler said, "to the comfort this Father gives his
children."

Fear not, for I am with you. Do not be dismayed.

*I am your God. I will strengthen you; I will help you;
I will uphold you with my victorious right hand. I am
holding you by your right hand—I, the Lord your God—
and I say to you, Do not be afraid; for I am here to help
you.*

*Despised though you are, fear not; for I will help you.
I am the Lord, your Redeemer; I am the Holy One.*

*When the poor and needy seek water and there is
none and their tongues are parched from thirst, then I
will answer when they cry to me. I will not ever forsake
them.*

*When you go through deep waters and great trouble, I
will be with you. When you go through rivers of difficulty, you will not drown! When you walk through the fire
of oppression, you will not be burned up—the flames will
not consume you.*

*As a reward for trusting me, I will preserve your life
and keep you safe.*

Old Sebastian stepped forward and said quietly,
"Does this loving Father really care for us? I believe,
yet I want to hear it over and over again. Please,
speak to us more about the love he has for those who
grieve."

Then the Unknown traveler set down The Book
and spoke words from it that he seemed to know by
heart.

Rest in the Lord; wait patiently for him to act.

Those who trust the Lord shall be given every blessing.

*It is good both to hope and wait quietly for the salva-
tion of the Lord.*

*We can rejoice when we run into problems and trials
for we know that they are good for us—they help us
learn to be patient.*

*Patience develops strength of character in us and helps
us trust God more each time we use it until finally our
hope and faith are strong and steady.*

*If we keep trusting God for something that has not
happened yet, it teaches us to wait patiently and confi-
dently.*

*When the way is rough, your patience has a chance to
grow. So let it grow, and do not try to squirm out of your*

problems. For when your patience is finally in full bloom, then you will be ready for anything, strong in character, full and complete.

God is our refuge and strength, a tested help in times of trouble. And so we need not fear, even if the world shatters into fragments, and the mountains crumble into the sea.

Then the Unknown Traveler heard the sound of a broken man weeping, and he knew that men could still weep because they had heard good things.

FORGIVENESS
AND MERCY

LARICE, a young woman who held a grudge against her sister, had listened to the words from The Book. Under the cool autumn sky she shivered, but not from the autumn breeze. She shivered as someone shivers when hearing something painfully but beautifully true.

Yet she felt inside herself a certain hardness. She wondered if anything could ever remove that hardness. She wondered if she could ever learn how to forgive.

She had never been a bold woman, but she stepped forward, and, almost murmuring, she spoke to the Unknown Traveler.

"You say things about the Maker of this world that touch me. I believe he must be great and mighty, a Maker of wondrous things. I believe he could transform an empty blackness into the universe. But could this same Maker show me how to heal a gap between one sister and another? How can we forgive each other?"

The Unknown Traveler knew that he could tell this woman about forgiveness by speaking of the forgiveness of a wayward son.

A man had two sons.

When the younger told his father, "I want my share of

your estate now, instead of waiting until you die!" his father agreed to divide his wealth between his sons.

A few days later this younger son packed all his belongings and took a trip to a distant land, and there wasted all his money on parties and prostitutes.

A great famine swept over the land, and he began to starve. He persuaded a local farmer to hire him to feed his pigs.

The boy became so hungry that even the pods he was feeding the swine looked good to him. And no one gave him anything.

When he finally came to his senses, he said to himself, "At home even the hired men have food enough and to spare, and here I am, dying of hunger! I will go home to my father and say, 'Father, I have sinned against both heaven and you, and am no longer worthy of being called your son. Please take me on as a hired man.'"

So he returned home to his father.

And while he was still a long distance away, his father saw him coming, and was filled with loving pity and ran and embraced him and kissed him.

His son said to him, "Father, I have sinned against heaven and you, and am not worthy of being called your son."

But his father said to the slaves, "Quick! Bring the finest robe in the house and put it on him. And a jeweled ring for his finger; and shoes! And kill the calf we have in the fattening pen. We must celebrate with a feast, for this son of mine was dead and has returned to life. He was lost and is found."

So the party began.

Then the Traveler read another story about the need to forgive.

The Kingdom of Heaven can be compared to a king who decided to bring his accounts up to date.

In the process, one of his debtors was brought in who owed him ten million.

But the man fell down before the king, his face in the dust, and said, "Oh, sir, be patient with me and I will pay it all." Then the king was filled with pity for him and released him and forgave his debt.

But when the man left the king, he went to a man who owed him two thousand and grabbed him by the throat and demanded instant payment.

The man fell down before him and begged him to give him a little time. "Be patient and I will pay it," he pled.

But his creditor would not wait. He had the man arrested and jailed until the debt would be paid in full.

Then the man's friends went to the king and told him what had happened.

And the king called before him the man he had forgiven and said, "You evil-hearted wretch! Here I forgave you all that tremendous debt, just because you asked me to—should you not have mercy on others, just as I had mercy on you?"

Then the angry king sent the man to the torture chamber until he had paid every last penny due.

So shall my heavenly Father do to you if you refuse to truly forgive your brothers.

Clarice listened closely to the story. So did Martin, who also had known the bitterness that comes from not forgiving.

The Unknown Traveler continued to read.

Your heavenly Father will forgive you if you forgive those who sin against you; but if you refuse to forgive them, he will not forgive you.

When you are praying, first forgive anyone you are holding a grudge against, so that your Father in heaven will forgive you your sins too.

Be gentle and ready to forgive; never hold grudges.

35

Remember, the Lord forgave you, so you must forgive others.

Do not repay evil for evil. Do not snap back at those who say unkind things about you.

Instead, pray for God's help for them, for we are to be kind to others, and God will bless us for it.

Do not rejoice when your enemy meets trouble. Let there be no gladness when he falls. Do not say, "Now I can pay him back for all his meanness to me!"

If your enemy is hungry, give him food! If he is thirsty, give him something to drink! This will make him feel ashamed of himself, and God will reward you.

Dear friends, never avenge yourselves. Leave that to God, for he has said that he will repay those who deserve it. Do not take the law into your own hands. Do not let evil get the upper hand but conquer evil by doing good.

Do not resist violence! If you are slapped on one cheek, turn the other too. If you are ordered to court, and your shirt is taken from you, give your coat too.

"You understand all of this, do you not?" asked the Unknown Traveler. "These truths are so simple. Think of how you could summarize them all." Then he began to read again from The Book.

Happy are the kind and merciful, for they shall be shown mercy.

Be kind to each other, tenderhearted, forgiving one another, just as God has forgiven you because you belong to Christ.

"You see," said the Traveler, "there is unbounded forgiveness for you. There are no limits on it at all. Once the Son of God had a question posed to him about whether there were indeed limits to forgiveness."

Peter came to him and asked, "Sir, how often should I forgive a brother who sins against me? Seven times?"

"No!" Jesus replied, "seventy times seven!"

"How hard this seems, yet so simple, really. But you must know that people always suffer for living the truth. So remember these words."

If someone mistreats you because you are a Christian, do not curse him; pray that God will bless him. Never pay back evil for evil.

"I have one more thing to read," said the Unknown Traveler. "It is something you should hope you will be able to say about yourselves someday. Listen closely."

We have blessed those who cursed us.
We have been patient with those who injured us.
We have replied quietly when evil things have been
*   said about us.*

Then Clarice closed her eyes and resolved to believe the truth and do the truth. And she no longer shivered, though the cool breeze blew through the willows on the square.

LOVE

As a mild breeze of autumn passed lazily over the square, some of the people pulled their wraps around them. It was late in the season, and the breeze was now of the shivering kind.

But one young couple, so taken with each other that they could scarce bear to shift their gaze from each other to the Unknown Traveler, did not feel the breeze at all, so warmed were they by the fire they had kindled in themselves.

The girl, though, had heard some of the Traveler's words, and without fully taking her eyes from the boy, said to the Traveler, "Love is the greatest thing in the world, is it not? Tell us more about love."

"Greatest, grandest, noblest, purest—how many words and images we could pile one on another, yet we would not do it justice," said the Unknown Traveler. "In truth, there are no words to define it. It is defined only by the source, God, and the Son of God. We know nothing of love unless we know of them. Man and woman cannot know true love for each other unless they know the tenderness of the Father for his children." Then he began to read from The Book.

He is like a father to us, tender and sympathetic to those who reverence him. For he knows we are but dust, and that our days are few and brief, like grass, like flowers, blown by the wind and gone forever. He will never completely take away his loving-kindness.

God showed his great love for us by sending Christ to die for us while we were still sinners. He loved us so much that even though we were spiritually dead and doomed by our sins, he gave us back our lives again when he raised Christ from the dead—only by his undeserved favor have we ever been saved—and lifted us up from the grave into glory along with Christ.

When the time came for the kindness and love of God our Savior to appear, then he saved us—not because we were good enough to be saved, but because of his kindness and pity—by washing away our sins and giving us the new joy of the indwelling Holy Spirit whom he poured out upon us with wonderful fullness—and all because of what Jesus Christ our Savior did.

God showed how much he loved us by sending his only Son into this wicked world to bring to us eternal life through his death. In this act we see what real love is: it is not our love for God, but his love for us when he sent his Son.

Some among the People of the Valley were puzzled by what the Traveler said about Jesus, the Son of God. But a few remembered hearing of how he had taught marvelous things, healed the sick, and then died like a criminal so that all people, failing to live as God had intended, would not have to die eternally. And the ones who remembered these things hoped that the Traveler would soon say more. Then the Traveler spoke to the young couple again.

"Ah, young ones, you stand there in the chill of autumn gleaming like stars, and seeing you is itself a delight. You will always remember these glory days, remember how the swan in the evening moved over the lake as you stood there at the water's edge, believing no two people had beheld such a sunset.

"Yet how much you have to learn of love, for the enchantment and the ardor wane when love is rooted in what we think is lovable. How quick we are to smile on what charms us, how quick to express our love for it. Yet the love of the Creator of this fallen world goes so much beyond that, for he showed that love is best when it is bestowed on what is not lovable. Page after page of The Book testifies to that kind of love, the love of a righteous God for people who are not righteous." Then he began to read again, so they would know how to respond to the love they did not deserve from God.

You must love God with all your heart, soul, and might.

What does the Lord your God require of you except to listen carefully to all he says to you, and to obey for your own good the commandments, and to love him, to be fair and just and merciful, and to walk humbly with your God, and to worship him with all your hearts and souls?

Love the Lord and follow his plan for your lives. Cling to him and serve him enthusiastically.

Be delighted with the Lord. Then he will give you all your heart's desires.

Oh, love the Lord, all of you who are his people; for the Lord protects those who are loyal to him, but harshly punishes all who haughtily reject him.

Seeing again the young couple, and knowing they would often murmur tender words to each other, the Traveler read these words of those whose love for God had erupted into song.

Lord, how I love you! For you have done such tremendous things for me.

Whom have I in heaven but you? And I desire no one on earth as much as you! My health fails; my spirits droop, yet God remains! He is the strength of my heart; he is mine forever!

Knowing the nature of people who have love billowing inside them, the Traveler spoke of that pleasure that comes from heeding and serving the one who is loved.

How I love your laws! How I enjoy your commands! "Come, come to me," I call to them, for I love them and will let them fill my life.

Nothing is perfect except your words. Oh, how I love them. I think about them all day long.

I love the Lord because he hears my prayers and answers them.

Because he bends down and listens, I will pray as long as I breathe!

Even the young couple, still unlettered in the world's lessons, understood these things. They knew that much love was manifested in asking—with that strange mingling of humility and intensity—for the lover's attention. And they knew that love was manifested as well in paying heed to the lover's counsel.

Cecilia, a woman not far past the prime of life, had long ago forgotten how to love her husband, and he had given her the same gift of unkindness. The woman could see the young couple standing there, and in her bitterness she did as the bitter often do and uttered words of painful truth.

"Sir," she said to the Traveler, "we have all known lovers so lost in their own universe that they cared for no one else. And we have all known people who claimed to be worshipers of God, yet these same people cared for no one besides those in their own

You will always
remember these glory days,
remember how the swan
in the evening moved
over the lake as you stood
there at the water's edge,
believing no two people had
beheld such a sunset.

circle. Is God pleased when people sing of their devotion to him and sneer at those around them?"

The Traveler knew that the woman already knew the answer to her question. Yet her words deserved a longer answer from The Book, and so he gave it to her.

Dear friends, let love be your greatest aim.

You must love others as much as yourself. If we love God, we will do whatever he tells us to. And he has told us from the very first to love each other.

Let us practice loving each other, for love comes from God and those who are loving and kind show that they are the children of God, and that they are getting to know him better. But if a person is not loving and kind, it shows that he does not know God—for God is love.

Since God loved us much, we surely ought to love each other too. For though we have never yet seen God, when we love each other God lives in us and his love within us grows ever stronger. And he has put his own Holy Spirit into our hearts as a proof to us that we are living with him and he with us.

And furthermore, we have seen with our own eyes and now tell all the world that God sent his Son to be their Savior. Anyone who believes and says that Jesus is the Son of God has God living in him, and he is living with God.

Now you can have real love for everyone because your souls have been cleansed from selfishness and hatred when you trusted Christ to save you. So see to it that you really do love each other warmly, with all your hearts.

Do not just pretend that you love others: really love them.

Hate what is wrong. Stand on the side of the good. For he who dislikes his brother is wandering in spiritual darkness and does not know where he is going, for the darkness has made him blind so that he cannot see the way.

The Traveler looked at Cecilia, the bitter woman, then at the young couple. "How unlike the way of this selfish world, to love one who is not lovable. When someone's face or heart is pleasing to you, you are drawn toward him like one who hears celestial music coming from behind a door. You will always want to open that door, wanting to be closer, to find love. But behind another door you hear discord, or foreign music that seems strange to you, and you walk the other way. Yet those doors too must be opened."

You should be like one big happy family, full of sympathy toward each other, loving one another with tender hearts and humble minds. Do not repay evil for evil. Do not snap back at those who say unkind things about you. Instead, pray for God's help for them, for we are to be kind to others, and God will bless us for it.

Pay all your debts except the debt of love for others—never finish paying that! For if you love them, you will be obeying all of God's laws, fulfilling all his requirements.

If you love your neighbor as much as you love yourself you will not want to harm or cheat him, or kill him or steal from him. And you will not sin with his wife or want what is his, or do anything else the Ten Commandments say is wrong. All ten are wrapped up in this one, to love your neighbor as you love yourself.

We know how much God loves us because we have felt his love and because we believe him when he tells us that he loves us dearly. God is love, and anyone who lives in love is living with God and God is living in him.

And as we live with Christ, our love grows more perfect and complete; so we will not be ashamed and

*embarrassed at the day of judgment, but can face him
with confidence and joy, because he loves us and we love
him too.*

*Love does no wrong to anyone. That is why it fully
satisfies all of God's requirements. It is the only law you
need.*

Because the Traveler knew that loving others was
painful and demanding, he continued with painful
words:

*Do you think you deserve credit for merely loving those
who love you? Even the godless do that! And if you do
good only to those who do you good—is that so wonderful? Even sinners do that much!*

*And if you lend money only to those who can repay
you, what good is that? Even the most wicked will lend
to their own kind for full return!*

*Love your enemies! Do good to them! Lend to them!
And do not be concerned about the fact that they will
not repay. Then your reward from heaven will be very
great, and you will truly be acting as sons of God: for he
is kind to the unthankful and to those who are very
wicked.*

"Dear friends," the Traveler said, "some of your
teachers have told you of animals and how they appear to show kindness to one another. And this is so,
for the One who set the world in motion and holds its
particles together—he infused his order with not only
harmony but also charity. But know this: No beast
and no bird spreads out a feast for its enemies. The
murderer may one day dine with the father of his
victim, because the father can forgive, as any man
can. No creature can do such things, none but the
man whose heart beats like the heart of God, pulsing
with those living words 'I forgive, I love, I forgive, I

love.' The beasts do not sin, but the beasts do not—cannot—forgive. And so they do not know fully the love of the forgiver for the forgiven." Then the Traveler read again.

Since you have been chosen by God who has given you this new kind of life, and because of his deep love and concern for you, you should practice tenderhearted mercy and kindness to others. Be gentle and ready to forgive; never hold grudges. Remember, the Lord forgave you, so you must forgive others.

Try to show as much compassion as your Father does. Whoever loves his fellow man is "walking in the light."

Now God can always point to us as examples of how very, very rich his kindness is, as shown in all he has done for us through Jesus Christ.

Martin was deeply moved by all the Traveler had said. "What you said before is true, Traveler. You said that love lies beyond all words. There is nothing more that could be said about it."

"Friend, you are right. Yet like all that is inexpressible, the ones who have encountered it will never hesitate to seek the words to express it. And perhaps the greatest words of all are these, written by one who knew how frail and empty words could be." And with that he began to read again.

If I had the gift of being able to speak in other languages without learning them, and could speak in every language there is in all of heaven and earth, but did not love others, I would only be making noise.

If I had the gift of prophecy and knew all about what is going to happen in the future, knew everything about everything, but did not love others, what good would it do?

Love is very patient and kind, never jealous or envi-

47

ous, never boastful or proud, never haughty or selfish or rude.

Love does not demand its own way. It is not irritable or touchy. It does not hold grudges and will hardly even notice when others do it wrong. It is never glad about injustice, but rejoices whenever truth wins out.

If you love someone you will be loyal to him no matter what the cost. You will always believe in him, always expect the best of him, and always stand your ground in defending him.

All the special gifts and powers from God will someday come to an end, but love goes on forever. Someday prophecy, and speaking in unknown languages, and special knowledge—these gifts will disappear.

Now we know so little, even with our special gifts, and the preaching of those most gifted is still so poor. But when we have been made perfect and complete, then the need for these inadequate special gifts will come to an end, and they will disappear.

There are three things that remain—faith, hope, and love—and the greatest of these is love.

Let love guide your life.

And with that he closed The Book for awhile, for it did not now seem right to speak anymore.

FRIENDSHIP

JARED and Edmund had been friends since boyhood. Now the two of them stood in the square, their hair much whiter and thinner than it was decades ago when they scrambled up the old mulberry trees in the Valley, giggling like fools, unashamed of their merriment.

But today the two were not standing together. They were on opposite sides of the square, and once when their eyes met they both looked away. The two old friends had quarreled weeks and weeks ago, and though the memory of the quarrel was fading, the bitter resentment that abides after quarrels was still there, lingering like the sullen smoke that hangs after a great fire has long passed.

For such as these—people who had known iron-clad love and were willing to throw it aside—the Traveler began to read from The Book.

David met Jonathan, the king's son, and there was an immediate bond of love between them. Jonathan swore to be his blood brother. Jonathan loved him as much as he loved himself.

"Dear people," the Traveler said, looking with compassion on Jared, "you may go to your graves debating the nature of love. But how often in the history of this tired, erring world has there ever been a love that endured and matured better than the best of friendships? The fiery love that takes possession of man and woman—what a delight it is while it burns! What joy in gazing into the eyes of another! Yet what compares with two pairs of eyes gazing in the same direction, fixed on the same goal? What compares with Jonathan, the king of Israel's noble son, and his love for David, the king to be? Does not every wife yearn for her husband to love her with such unwearying love? Hear the words of a man with his heart in tatters over a friend who died."

How I weep for you, my brother Jonathan. How much I loved you! And your love for me was deeper than the love of women!

Many of the People of the Valley had known Jared and Edmund for years, and the two men's quarrel was a thing for gossips to feed on. But no one who heard the Traveler's words could help but feel for the two old men and the love that had seen them through sunshine and shadow, fountains of laughter and torrents of tears. And the two old men themselves ached as the Traveler began to read again.

A true friend is always loyal, and a brother is born to help in time of need.

There are "friends" who pretend to be friends, but there is a friend who sticks closer than a brother.

Wounds from a friend are better than kisses from an enemy.

Friendly suggestions are as pleasant as perfume.

A friendly discussion is as stimulating as the sparks that fly when iron strikes iron.

50

Edmund's son was standing near his father, and he leaned forward and began to whisper in his ear. "Father, I don't understand this senseless argument you've had." But before he could say more, the old man hushed him with a firm wave of his hand. Edmund was listening to the Traveler, but his pride gripped him and murmured, "Wait, wait, and let the offending party make the first step toward reconciling." And as men love to listen to pride, Edmund listened. Yet he was not sure who the offending party was, himself or Jared, or whether it mattered at all.

Then the Unknown Traveler read these words about the peculiar efficiency of love:

Two can accomplish more than twice as much as one, for the results can be much better. If one falls, the other pulls him up; but if a man falls when he is alone, he is in trouble.

On a cold night, two under the same blanket gain warmth from each other, but how can one be warm alone? And one standing alone can be attacked and defeated, but two can stand back-to-back and conquer; three is even better, for a triple-braided cord is not easily broken.

The Traveler looked at Edmund's face, which was now set like a stone, made stern by pride. Then he read these words:

Hatred stirs old quarrels, but love overlooks insults. Love forgets mistakes; nagging about them parts the best of friends.

How wonderful it is, how pleasant, when brothers live in harmony!

Never abandon a friend. Love each other with brotherly affection and take delight in honoring each other.

Then Jared marveled in his heart that he and his companion of so many decades had so quickly forgotten how to honor each other. Jared was old, and he remembered his aged father speaking these words from The Book:

One should be kind to a fainting friend.

And, ah, how often the constant Edmund had proved himself to be kind.

Then Jared recalled these other words his father had said to him:

A mirror reflects a man's face, but what he is really like is shown by the kind of friends he chooses.

Jared had never regretted having Edmund by his side. For in more than seventy years of life he had had friends richer, more influential, more learned, quicker of wit, more well-appointed in their dress, more gracious in their manner. But never had he taken a more loyal man to his heart. And as he came to know loyalty by seeing loyalty, others saw the two of them as a standard of loyalty. So his father's words— the words from The Book—had been proved true. Anyone who knew Jared would know what Edmund was like, and those who knew Edmund knew Jared. And to know either was to know fidelity.

Then Jared remembered, as the aged so easily remember words spoken in their childhood, other words from The Book. But these were the words of a man whose friends had failed him when he was in the dust:

My friends scoff at me, but I pour out my tears to God, pleading that he will listen.

And Jared pitied that poor man, for he knew that he could not endure Edmund scoffing at him. But this had never happened, and for this he was thankful.

As a tiny bead of shame dropped onto the two men's pride and began to erode it like acid, the Traveler read these words spoken by the Son of God to his beloved disciples:

You are my friends. The greatest love is shown when a man lays down his life for his friends.

And while some of the People of the Valley puzzled at these words, knowing how uncommon it must be for anyone to show so much love, Jared and Edmund considered that they had both known such a man. And though neither had ever been called to lay down his life for the other, neither doubted that it could be done if it must be done.

Stubbornness is a force based on folly, and when folly is seen for what it is, the stubbornness gladly melts. And pride, diamond-hard though it is, gives way meekly to love, which in the end is harder than anything else, though its outside is supple and warm.

When the Traveler looked at the spot where Jared had been standing, no one was there. Edmund, likewise, was not where he had been. And in the mass of people there they could not be seen for the time being. But the Traveler did not doubt that in only a moment the two would be drawing very near to each other.

Some of the People of the Valley pondered the words the Son of God had said to his well-loved followers. And some began to understand what a great compliment had been paid to those disciples.

MARRIAGE

A COUPLE many years married, Clement and Lenore, stood side by side in the square as the Unknown Traveler spoke. He could tell from looking at them that they had lived many days and nights together, sharing words of compassion and fondness, but also sharing words that cut like daggers. And he knew that other husbands and wives had likewise learned to wound with words and with looks. So the Traveler began to speak The Book's words about why a man and woman would ever want to join together for life.

The Lord God said, "It is not good for man to be alone; I will make a companion for him, a helper suited to his needs."

So the Lord God formed from the soil every kind of animal and bird, and brought them to the man to see what he would call them; and whatever he called them, that was their name. But still there was no proper helper for the man.

Then the Lord God caused the man to fall into a deep sleep, and took one of his ribs and closed up the place from which he had removed it, and made the rib into a woman, and brought her to the man.

"This is it!" Adam exclaimed. "She is part of my own bone and flesh! Her name is 'woman' because she was

*taken out of a man." This explains why a man leaves his
father and mother and is joined to his wife in such a way
that the two become one person.*

*Remember that in God's plan men and women need
each other.*

The Traveler could tell from Clement's tired eyes
that he understood the words. Yet Clement's face also
showed that he had long ago ceased to see his wife as a
good companion. And Lenore, too, showed in her
face that her early love had faded. Then the Traveler
spoke again, looking intently at the women in the
square.

*The man who finds a wife finds a good thing; she is a
blessing to him from the Lord. A worthy wife is her husband's joy and crown; the other kind corrodes his
strength and tears down everything he does.*

*Wives, fit in with your husbands' plans. Sarah, for in-
stance, obeyed her husband Abraham, honoring him as
head of the house. And if you do the same, you will be
following in her steps like good daughters and doing what
is right.*

*Charm can be deceptive and beauty does not last, but
a woman who fears and reverences God shall be greatly
praised. Do not be concerned about the outward beauty
that depends on jewelry, or beautiful clothes, or hair ar-
rangement.*

*Be beautiful inside, in your hearts, with the lasting
charm of a gentle and quiet spirit which is so precious to
God. That kind of deep beauty was seen in the saintly
women of old, who trusted God and fitted in with their
husbands' plans.*

As he spoke, Lenore remembered how their home,
so peaceful in the early years of a long marriage, had
so often seemed like a battleground. She remembered

the part she had played in the strife. And the Traveler's words cut her, though it was the kind of cut that brings healing. The Traveler spoke again, looking first at Clement, then at many of the other men gathered there, knowing that they had forgotten the gentleness of their younger days.

Live happily with the woman you love through the fleeting days of life, for the wife God gives you is your best reward down here for all your earthly toil. Drink from your own well, my son—be faithful and true to your wife.

Be happy, yes, rejoice in the wife of your youth. Let her tender embrace satisfy you. Let her love alone fill you with delight. A man must love his wife as a part of himself; and the wife must see to it that she deeply respects her husband—obeying, praising and honoring him.

You husbands must be careful of your wives, being thoughtful of their needs and honoring them. Remember that you and your wife are partners in receiving God's blessings.

Husbands, show the same kind of love to your wives as Christ showed to the Church. That is how husbands should treat their wives, loving them as parts of themselves. For since a man and his wife are now one, a man is really doing himself a favor and loving himself when he loves his wife!

There were also in the crowd two people, a husband and a wife, who were not standing side by side. The husband, Nicholas, and the wife, Monica, had abandoned all hope for their marriage. The vows they had made when their young eyes had shimmered with love were now regarded as a hindrance. They intended to dissolve what they had once sworn could never be dissolved. And while they thought of divorce, they were not the only couple to think this way. This the Traveler knew, for it was true everywhere. So he spoke these words to the People of the Valley:

In God's wise plan, when you married, the two of you became one person in his sight.

Therefore guard your passions! Keep faith with the wife of your youth. For the Lord hates divorce.

From the very first God made man and woman to be joined together permanently in marriage. Therefore a man is to leave his father and mother and he and his wife are united so that they are no longer two, but one.

No man may separate what God has joined together. When a man divorces his wife to marry someone else, he commits adultery against her. And if a wife divorces her husband and remarries, she, too, commits adultery.

At this last word one woman winced, though she knew the husband she loved so dearly would never divorce her. But she knew that he had come to scoff at his vow of fidelity. And a wave of pain washed over her. Then the Traveler spoke.

Honor your marriage and its vows, and be pure; for God will surely punish all those who are immoral or commit adultery.

Why delight yourself with prostitutes, embracing what is not yours? For God is closely watching you, and he weighs carefully everything you do.

One young man, a tall, bearded scholar, stood by, nodding his head in agreement, for he had seen people wounded by divorce. And though he knew the pains of unhappy homes where marriage had become lifeless and empty, he knew also of the bitterness of marriage dissolved. He had even asked himself many times if perhaps it might be best not to marry at all.

But the fear of living alone in a world of married couples gnawed at him. His eyes widened as the Traveler began to speak again.

If you do not marry, it is good.

If a man has the willpower not to marry and decides that he does not need to and will not, he has made a wise decision. But usually it is best to be married, each man having his own wife, and each woman having her own husband, because otherwise you might fall into sin.

I am not saying you must marry; but you certainly may if you wish. I wish everyone could get along without marrying, just as I do.

But we are not all the same. God gives some the gift of a husband or wife, and others he gives the gift of being able to stay happily unmarried. I want you to do whatever will help you serve the Lord best.

The young man heard these words and took comfort in knowing that he could please God whether he chose to marry or not.

As the Traveler looked around the square, he could see the faces of eager youth, some of them anticipating the joys of marriage, some of them already sure that marriage would inevitably lapse into a tedious ritual, to be followed by other marriages that would also fade and fail. The Traveler could see older couples whose lives had indeed become tedious. Yet his gaze rested for a time on one elderly couple that seemed almost to be looking at him with the same pair of eyes. And he spoke to the wife in a soft voice. "Old woman, do you ever thank Almighty God for this man by your side?"

The old woman, though feeble of voice, did not hesitate for a second. "Indeed, indeed. After all the tribulations have been counted and weighed, they account for so much less than the days and nights of comfort. I have regrets in this life, but I do not regret that I bound up my life with this man's life."

Then the old man spoke. "Nor do I."

And at that the Traveler smiled, knowing that the words he read from The Book would not be wasted so long as this venerable pair and others like them lived to give the words meaning.

CHILDREN

WHILE the Unknown Traveler was speaking of marriage, the Valley's children played in the square, the same as children have done for centuries upon centuries. The Traveler knew well the pain that children could bring to their families. Yet he also knew the incomparable delight a child's smile could bring to even the most jaded heart. He looked at a small boy—a wide-eyed boy with unruly hair—tugging anxiously on his father's sleeve, and then he spoke these words:

Children are a gift from God; they are his reward.
Children born to a young man are like sharp arrows to defend him. Happy is the man who has his quiver full of them.

The Traveler could see the small boy had moved to the side of an older man, a man who placed a wrinkled but loving hand on the boy's head. He knew this was the child's grandfather, and he said this:

An old man's grandchildren are his crowning glory.

Then the Traveler read this story of how the Son of God cared for little children:

Once when some mothers were bringing their children to Jesus to bless them, the disciples shooed them away, telling them not to bother him.

But when Jesus saw what was happening he was very much displeased with his disciples and said to them, "Let the children come to me, for the Kingdom of God belongs to such as they. Do not send them away! I tell you as seriously as I know how that anyone who refuses to come to God as a little child will never be allowed into his Kingdom."

Then he took the children into his arms and placed his hands on their heads and he blessed them.

Then he spoke these words, words he knew would chafe those who had no real love for life, born or unborn:

"Listen, People of the Valley. Life is a good gift from your Creator. Cherish life, guard it. Hear The Book's words about the beginning of life and children."

You made all the delicate, inner parts of my body, and knit them together in my mother's womb. Thank you for making me so wonderfully complex! It is amazing to think about. Your workmanship is marvelous—and how well I know it.

You were there while I was being formed in utter seclusion! You saw me before I was born and scheduled each day of my life before I began to breathe. Every day was recorded in your Book!

The Traveler could see a small boy, a lonely, sullen boy, sitting on the ground, tracing meaningless patterns with a stick he was holding. The boy's father and mother were whispering to each other, clearly paying no heed to either the Traveler or their boy.

The Traveler knew such parents well. He knew they were so occupied with their own affairs that they gave little thought or time to the child they had brought into the world. He knew that they would give the child little guidance as he matured. And they would cover up their own laziness and selfishness with empty words about how a child should be allowed to choose his own path and decide things for himself. And for them the Traveler read these words from The Book:

If you refuse to discipline your son, it proves you do not love him; for if you love him you will be prompt to punish him. Discipline your son in his early years while there is hope. If you do not you will ruin his life.

A youngster's heart is filled with rebellion, but punishment will drive it out of him. Scolding and spanking a child helps him to learn. Left to himself, he brings shame to his mother. Teach a child to choose the right path, and when he is older he will remain upon it.

Happy is the man with a level-headed son; sad the mother of a rebel.

But on the other side of the square was a sad-faced girl, a girl whose pale eyes had been reddened with tears, not just today, but often. She, the Traveler could tell, was already full of anger and resentment. She did not lack for a mother's or father's discipline. What she lacked was a home where wisdom and self-control tempered strictness, adding love to the correcting hand. For the parents of such a child as this the Traveler lifted these words of The Book:

Do not keep on scolding and nagging your children, making them angry and resentful. Rather, bring them up with the loving discipline the Lord himself approves, with suggestions and godly advice.

Amelia, a young woman whose face expressed a wisdom that many older people did not possess, stepped forward, all the while holding the hand of her young son.

"Sir," she said, "everything you say is true. But I have a friend whose daughter has broken her heart. She and her husband did what they could, and the other children turned out well. Yet one child did not. Are we alone responsible for what our children do? Have you nothing to say to the children themselves? Should they not have to bear some of the load?"

Her piercing eyes looked directly at the Traveler, and he knew this woman would not move until she had a reply. And he gave this answer from The Book—not to Amelia, and not to the other fathers and mothers, but to the children:

Children, obey your parents; this is the right thing to do because God has placed them in authority over you.

Honor your father and mother. This is the first of God's Ten Commandments that ends with a promise. And this is the promise: that if you honor your father and mother, yours will be a long life, full of blessing.

Obey your father and your mother. Take to heart all of their advice; keep in mind everything they tell you.

Every day and all night long their counsel will lead you and save you from harm; when you wake up in the morning, let their instructions guide you into the new day. For their advice is a beam of light directed into the dark corners of your mind to warn you of danger and to give you a good life.

After reading this, the Unknown Traveler looked into Amelia's eyes and saw that she was satisfied with the answer.

"Young woman," he said, "love that child you are holding by the hand there. All of you fathers and

Are we alone responsible
for what our children do?
Have you nothing to say
to the children themselves?
Should they not have to
bear some of the load?

mothers, listen. Be that beam of light spoken of in The Book. And you children, follow the light. No man, woman, or child can do anything better or wiser than this: Follow the light."

Perched on her father's shoulders, a little girl pulled playfully but gently at his beard, and his fingers intertwined with hers.

KNOWLEDGE

A MAN named Milo was a teacher, much loved by generations of students. For five decades Milo had taken the young ones of the Valley to a ridge and said to them, "All of this is yours, and greater things besides, if you have knowledge. You were born to know. This is what lifts you up from the mud and separates you from the beasts. There is nothing in this galaxy with its unnumbered stars that you cannot measure and count and dissect. And it may be someday that I will tell my students that the stars are, indeed, now numbered. This is your destiny. Know, analyze, control. Remind each other that the fences and the walls within your minds must be demolished. And if some part of the universe builds a wall around itself, shutting you out, tear down that wall."

Now Milo was in the square that day, listening to the Unknown Traveler, pleased to hear that someone was valiant for truth.

Milo spoke to the Traveler. "Sir, I have spent seventy years tracking down the truth, and fifty of those years guiding others toward it. Surely this Book, this treasure you have unearthed after all these centuries, will give us knowledge as we have never known."

"Knowledge indeed," said the Traveler, perceiving

67

what sort of man he spoke to. "If knowledge had weight, you could not lift The Book. If it fell upon you, it would crush you like a boulder crushing a flea. And now I will read you The Book's first tale of knowledge. It concerns the first man and woman in the world. The loving Creator, having formed them from the dust and placed them in the loveliest of gardens, gave them all that could be desired. Yet they desired more. The fruit given them to eat was not enough. Like rebellious children, they ate from a tree called the Tree of Knowledge, a tree whose fruit the Lord had denied to them. And in doing this they changed forever that blessed state, the state of perfect harmony and perfect innocence, where they were naked and vulnerable yet not ashamed."

The serpent was the craftiest of all the creatures the Lord God had made. The serpent came to the woman. "Really?" he asked. "None of the fruit in the garden? God says you must not eat any of it?"

"Of course we may eat it," the woman told him. "It is only the fruit from the tree at the center of the garden that we are not to eat. God says we must not eat it or even touch it, or we will die."

"That is a lie!" the serpent hissed. "You will not die! God knows very well that the instant you eat it you will become like him, for your eyes will be opened—you will be able to distinguish good from evil!"

The woman was convinced. How lovely and fresh looking it was! And it would make her so wise! So she ate some of the fruit and gave some to her husband, and he ate it too. And as they ate it, suddenly they became aware of their nakedness, and were embarrassed. So they strung fig leaves together to cover themselves.

That evening they heard the sound of the Lord God walking in the garden. And they hid themselves among the trees. The Lord God called to Adam, "Why are you hiding?"

And Adam replied, "I heard you coming and did not want you to see me naked. So I hid."

"Who told you you were naked?" the Lord God asked. "Have you eaten fruit from the tree I warned you about?"

"Yes," Adam admitted, "but it was the woman you gave me who brought me some, and I ate it."

To Adam, God said, "Because you listened to your wife and ate the fruit when I told you not to, I have placed a curse upon the soil. All your life you will struggle to extract a living from it. All your life you will sweat to master it, until your dying day.

"Then you will return to the ground from which you came. For you were made from the ground, and to the ground you will return."

Milo blushed at this—not for himself, but for the Traveler. *How,* Milo said in his heart, *could this man stand before the people and read such mindless folk tales?*

Then Milo spoke aloud. "Do you want us to believe that we offend the God of heaven by seeking to be wise? I have taken a thousand students under my wing and shown them that God desires that we grow, learn, expand, grasp. And the God you speak of in your tale is not that same God. What sort of cruel Ruler would deny us what our minds can grasp?" And several of the People of the Valley who had loved Milo and gained from his instruction nodded in agreement. A few wandered back to their homes, full of the quiet indignity that some scholars wear so well. They were not inclined to bluster, for they believed only fools raved at other fools.

A young woman named Vivian had learned much from Milo, and she came to his defense. "What our revered teacher says is true," she said with proper politeness, though the edges of her soft words had nettles. "Surely the One you say is the Source of Truth would not treat his creatures so."

The Traveler paused. This was not the first occasion when a listener had balked at the ageless story. "Were you not listening? The curse put upon man was not for seeking knowledge, but for seeking to be like God. A creature—much loved, much gifted by his Maker, endowed with such faculties, blessed with the bounty of a world unspoiled—that creature wanted to be more than a creature. The man, made from the dust, wanted to forget his beginning."

The Traveler then sighed, seeing that even the wise disciples of Milo lacked so much understanding. "Beloved People of the Valley," he began, "surely you have seen that though you pile fact upon fact, making towers of them, making mountain ranges of them, you end by standing on them and seeing that there are cloud-shrouded mountains further in the distance. When you swallow a goblet full of knowledge, you then see that it came from a bottomless vat. Consider, then, these words from one of the wisest men who ever lifted up his eyes to consider this world:"

I was king of Israel, living in Jerusalem. And I applied myself to search for understanding about everything in the universe.

I said to myself, "Look, I am better educated than any of the kings before me. I have greater wisdom and knowledge." So I worked hard to be wise instead of foolish— but now I realize that even this was like chasing the wind. For the more my wisdom, the more my grief; to increase knowledge only increases distress.

Then the Unknown Traveler said, "The wise one, the king of Israel, had every pleasure open to him.

And you learn from his words that pursuit of knowledge is no grander or nobler than the childish pursuit of pleasure. If you do not feel your vanities pricked by his confession, at least heed the words of the Lord himself."

Where were you when I laid the foundations of the earth? Tell me, if you know so much.

Do you know how its dimensions were determined, and who did the surveying? What supports its foundations, and who laid its cornerstone, as the morning stars sang together and all the angels shouted for joy?

Who decreed the boundaries of the seas when they gushed from the depths? Who clothed them with clouds and thick darkness, and barred them by limiting their shores, and said, '"Thus far and no farther shall you come, and here shall your proud waves stop!"'?

Have you ever once commanded the morning to appear, and caused the dawn to rise in the east? Have you ever told the daylight to spread to the ends of the earth, to end the night's wickedness? Have you ever robed the dawn in red, and disturbed the haunts of wicked men and stopped the arm raised to strike?

Have you explored the springs from which the seas come, or walked in the sources of their depths? Has the location of the gates of Death been revealed to you? Do you realize the extent of the earth? Tell me about it if you know! Where does the light come from, and how do you get there? Or tell me about the darkness. Where does it come from? Can you find its boundaries, or go to its source? But of course you know all this! For you were born before it was all created, and you are so very experienced!

Have you visited the treasuries of the snow, or seen where hail is made and stored? Where is the path to the distribution point of light? Where is the home of the east wind? Who dug the valleys for the torrents of rain? Who laid out the path for the lightning, causing the rain to fall upon the barren deserts, so that the parched and barren ground is satisfied with water, and tender grass springs up?

Has the rain a father? Where does dew come from? Who is the mother of the ice and frost?

Can you hold back the stars? Can you restrain Orion or Pleiades? Can you ensure the proper sequence of the seasons? Do you know the laws of the universe and how the heavens influence the earth? Can you shout to the clouds and make it rain? Can you make lightning appear and cause it to strike as you direct it?

Who gives intuition and instinct? Who is wise enough to number all the clouds? Who can tilt the water jars of heaven, when everything is dust and clods?

Then the Traveler said, "Even if you knew every corner of this boundless world, even if you had charted and mapped and recorded every line and point of it, what would you have done, then? If you counted every grain of sand and numbered every feather on every bird that ever flew, would you be any more like the One who made the tides and sprinkled the skies with owls and falcons? Measurer is not Maker, and surveyor is not Sovereign. Yet how you delight in knowing, knowing, knowing, as though the substance there within your skulls had been placed there for nothing more than assuring itself that omniscience was within its reach."

Martin was listening to all this, remembering fondly how Milo had showed him the beating heart of an injured sparrow he nestled in his hand. And he and the other children had been delighted, running home to tell their parents what they had seen. Yet Martin had sat on the hillside only yesterday, a man perplexed and more than slightly hungry for the

Truth. Now he believed that Milo, the wise and be-loved Milo, had not pointed them toward truth—the Truth—but to will-o'-the-wisps, to bubbles that now burst. And he swallowed, and down his throat went regret. It was not regret that he had learned so much about the world and its workings, but that the Framer of the world had not been studied or known or thanked for the variety and the order of his inven-tion. And now he understood the story of the first man and woman, who chose to grasp for God's posi-tion and not to grasp for God himself.

Martin's youngest son was one of Milo's pupils. The son admired and respected his teacher, as Martin himself had done. The son, who was standing beside his father, looked into the weathered face of Milo, then spoke to the Traveler. "Sir, we have been taught from the cradle that we were to learn all we could. Is it wrong to do so?"

The Traveler smiled. "Young one, learn all you can. But know that you cannot possibly learn every-thing. Some things are less worthy of your mind than others. And know that some are most worthy of all. The Great Being who made everything to be—surely he is most worthy of your attentions." And at that time Milo and the young woman Vivian left the square, talking to each other as they left. The Travel-er watched them go, then read these words:

If anyone thinks he knows all the answers, he is just showing his ignorance. But the person who truly loves God is the one who is open to God's knowledge.

It is not mere age that makes men wise. Rather, it is the spirit in a man, the breath of the Almighty which makes him intelligent.

Stop fooling yourselves. If you count yourself above average in intelligence, as judged by this world's stan-

dards, you had better put this all aside and be a fool rather than let it hold you back from the true wisdom from above.

For the wisdom of this world is foolishness to God. He is not impressed by the world's wisest men! Woe to those who are wise and shrewd in their own eyes!

"People of the Valley, loved by God, if anyone asked you to bring forth evidence of the wise ones' blessings to their fellow creatures, what would you bring? With all its delights, its tantalizing notions, its poetry, its ability to provoke both laughter and tears, knowledge by itself appears weak and unfulfilled. For since the world began spinning the philosophers and scholars are no more inclined than the village idiots to lift up the fallen and nurse the dying. When the helpless scream in desperation, the sages retreat as swiftly as the dunces. Love is as likely to set in kind motion the hands of an utter fool as the hands of the academy's master."

A small boy sat near the feet of his father, who was listening earnestly to the Traveler. The Traveler looked at the boy's wide brown eyes and the pale unlined forehead. And he said to the boy's father, "Pray every morning and every night, and at every hour throughout the day, that your son will love God so dearly that he will call him 'Father' as freely as he uses the word for you. Pray that even if this boy learns nothing else, he will honor the one Being most deserving of honor." Then he read these words:

May you be able to feel and understand, as all God's children should, how long, how wide, how deep, and how high his love really is; and to experience this love for yourselves, though it is so great that you will never see the end of it or fully know or understand it. And so at last you will be filled up with God himself.

74

Oh, what a wonderful God we have! How great are his wisdom and knowledge and riches! How impossible it is for us to understand his decisions and his methods!

Who among us can know the mind of the Lord? Who knows enough to be his counselor and guide? And who could ever offer to the Lord enough to induce him to act? For everything comes from God alone. Everything lives by his power, and everything is for his glory. To him be glory evermore.

When he had read those words, a young woman whose limbs sometimes shook uncontrollably and whose head constantly nodded said in a loud voice, "Glory evermore!"

Martin's son tugged on his father's sleeve and said, "That's the feeble-minded girl who cannot read. And she still plays with dolls."

And Martin said to his son, "If those of us whose minds are whole and vigorous do not praise God joyfully, then it is we who are feeble-minded." Then the two of them heard a simple-hearted giggle from the girl, and Martin wondered if it was her way of praising the Creator.

THE SELF

$\mathcal{A}$ YOUNG woman named Candice lived in the Valley, as did her mother, and the two loved each other much and quarreled much. And she saw, as every grown child does, her mother's imperfections clearly. At times Candice loved her mother without questioning. And at times she would blame the ills of the world on her mother's failings.

The Unknown Traveler knew that such things occurred in the Valley, for they occurred everywhere. Children were wise enough to see their father's and mother's errors, yet cheerfully blind to their own. If a flood came in the child's life, it was because the parent had summoned up the clouds.

But the Traveler also knew how parents sometimes caused, though without intention, their children to become vain and self-absorbed. And they did so in the name of love, a name used to cover up much of the world's folly. So for generation after generation parent and child never so fully unite as in this one endeavor, the creation of perplexed and thoughtless children, children who learn only with difficulty that they are not the axis of the universe.

Candice, who was regarded by her friends as lacking in confidence, often complained of the lack of encouragement her mother had given her. She was certain that other children had received their fair share, while she had not. She believed this had engendered a lack of respect for herself. And since her mother was standing near her, and since the Traveler was there in the square to lead the people to the Truth, Candice believed that he would serve then and there to convict her mother of her defects.

"Sir," she said, "you tell us that our love for God is a sublime thing. But is it not right to love ourselves? We have all known the agony of hating ourselves, believing we were of no value, believing our few virtues paled next to our shortcomings, believing our minds and passions had no capacity for greatness. If some of this world's ills are due to our treason in not saluting the Governor of the cosmos, then surely some are due to that disabling treason of despising ourselves."

Many of Candice's friends nodded. And even a few parents nodded, for some willingly accepted guilt for their children's lack of self-love.

The Traveler held up The Book and said calmly, "Here are the words. Surely you all remember them. Humankind was made in the image of God, upright, pure. Your first parents tried to be like God, and ever afterward the harmony they first possessed has eluded you. Yet the sacred image in you is not erased, blurred though it is." Then the Traveler began to read.

O Lord our God, the majesty and glory of your name fills all the earth and overflows the heavens.

When I look up into the night skies and see the work of your fingers—the moon and the stars you have made—I cannot understand how you can bother with mere puny man, to pay any attention to him!

And yet you have made him only a little lower than

the angels, and placed a crown of glory and honor upon his head.

You have put him in charge of everything you made. Everything is put under his authority: all sheep and oxen, and wild animals too, the birds and fish, and all the life in the sea.

"Do these words lift this burden you claim to have? This weight of self-loathing you claim to sweat beneath—is it dispelled by hearing that the Lord God still gives man, sinful though he is, dominion over this world? Is this all you wished to hear, or would you like to hear more of the Truth?" Then he read again.

The heart is the most deceitful thing there is, and desperately wicked. No one can really know how bad it is! Only the Lord knows!

The Lord looks down from heaven on all mankind to see if there are any who are wise, who want to please God. But no, all have strayed away; all are rotten with sin. Not one is good, not one!

Claiming themselves to be wise without God, they became utter fools instead. And then, instead of worshiping the glorious, ever-living God, they took wood and stone and made idols for themselves, carving them to look like mere birds and animals and snakes and puny men.

So it was that when they gave God up and would not even acknowledge him, God gave them up to doing everything their evil minds could think of. Their lives became full of every kind of wickedness and sin, of greed and hate, envy, murder, fighting, lying, bitterness, and gossip.

These wicked men, so proud and haughty, seem to think that God is dead. They would not think of looking for him! They boast that neither God nor man can ever keep them down.

*Their mouths are full of profanity and lies and fraud.
They are always boasting of their evil plans. They lurk in
dark alleys of the city and murder passersby. Like lions
they crouch silently, waiting to pounce upon the poor.
Like hunters they catch their victims in their traps.*

*The unfortunate are overwhelmed by their superior
strength and fall beneath their blows. "God is not watching," they say to themselves; "he'll never know!"*

Only a fool would say to himself, "There is no God."

A certain bright-eyed young man, a friend of Candice, said to the Traveler, "Sir, you speak to us of
extremes. There are indeed wicked people walking
the globe. But most of us here are reasonable folk,
pleased to work for our livings, visit those we love,
rear our children, and harm no one. We tend our own
gardens. And if we wake at night, feeling a vague
pain gnawing in us, it is not guilt over our crimes. It is
contempt for ourselves. And why that contempt is in
us we cannot explain. But we know it is wrong."

"Are you so certain? How do you think you appear
to the Creator when you come before him, honoring
yourselves?" Then the Traveler read them this story
told by the Son of God:

*Two men went to the Temple to pray. One was a proud,
self-righteous Pharisee, and the other a cheating tax collector. The proud Pharisee "prayed" this prayer:*

*"Thank God, I am not a sinner like everyone else, es-
pecially like that tax collector over there! For I never
cheat, I do not commit adultery, I go without food twice
a week, and I give to God a tenth of everything I earn."*

*But the corrupt tax collector stood at a distance and
dared not even lift his eyes to heaven as he prayed, but
beat upon his chest in sorrow, exclaiming, "God, be merciful to me, a sinner." I tell you, this sinner, not the*

Pharisee, returned home forgiven! For the proud shall be humbled, but the humble shall be honored.

"Dear People of the Valley, though you were made in the image of God, you are a fallen, marred race. Do you understand this? Inside you mingle angel and beast together, and the two are at war in even those who appear principled. And even when you have cast out the grosser sins from your lives—murder, theft, and all that are easily visible to observers—then you are still clinging to the pet sin, the sin of the righteous, which is pride. And yet you come to me, wanting me to read you words affirming your pride and self-love.

"I cannot read such affirmations from The Book, for they are not there. These pages will not encourage your self-lauding. For the God of heaven knows your hearts, and he knows that no man or woman will find joy in being 'I' unless there is a 'they' to look down upon. A person by himself or a group banding together—when human beings begin to applaud their own goodness and their own uniqueness, then they begin to hiss someone else's loathsomeness. There is no pride without prejudice. When you announce to the world 'I am good' or 'We are good,' you announce your contempt for someone else. You wish this was not so, but it is so. Do not think you can cast out your self-hate and fill up the void with self-love. You are impotent in this."

The Traveler could in some eyes see a hint of gloom, and in some there was the low fire of indignation. He knew these words were of no comfort, and he did not wish to leave the people empty. So he said, "The Book will not give you what you asked for—not in regard to your pride. But I will read something else to you." And he said to them these words from the Son of God:

If you are invited to a wedding feast, do not always head for the best seat.

Do this instead—start at the foot. For everyone who tries to honor himself shall be humbled; and he who humbles himself shall be honored.

The more lowly your service to others, the greater you are. To be the greatest, be a servant. But those who think themselves great shall be disappointed and humbled; and those who humble themselves shall be exalted.

Then the bright-eyed young man said to the Traveler, "Is this the cure for all our discomfort? If we act humbly, have we fulfilled our duty to God and quieted our insides?" And he asked this with hesitation, for he was still unsure of the rightness of humility.

The Traveler shook his head. "Humility is in human eyes a muddy stone, but a polished diamond in the eyes of God. Yet how perverse your hearts are— you who ask me to sanction your love of self. There are humble men and women who lock their doors at night, kneeling before the Almighty, so proud of their humility that it hangs like a thick veil between them and the Captain of earth and heaven. Pride prevents the discernment of pride. You cannot see your own eyes because you are inside them, looking outward. So it is with pride. It hides itself well. And so do a thousand other petty sins."

Then the Traveler read these words of a sinful man who begged to be given clear eyes:

How can I ever know what sins are lurking in my heart? Cleanse me from these hidden faults. And keep me from deliberate wrongs; help me to stop doing them. Only then can I be free of guilt and innocent.

"How are we to be cleansed?" asked Candice. "You have made it clear to us that we are powerless to help ourselves. You preach to us a philosophy of dismay."

"That is what it is," said the Traveler. "That is the purpose of The Book. It will lead you to despair. You want me to tell you you are good. I tell you instead that you are fallen, marred. I tell you that your own attempts to press the seal of validity on your existence will come to nothing. I tell you that your restlessness comes not from lack of self-love, but from lack of reality. For until you face yourselves in clear mirrors and acknowledge your fallenness, you will have sleepless nights. Consider the words of one of the holy ones, a man on fire for God. Hear his confession of his weakness."

I do not understand myself at all, for I really want to do what is right, but I cannot. I do what I do not want to—what I hate. I know perfectly well that what I am doing is wrong, and my bad conscience proves that I agree with these laws I am breaking.

But I cannot help myself, because I'm no longer doing it. It is sin inside me that is stronger than I am that makes me do these evil things.

I know I am rotten through and through so far as my old sinful nature is concerned. No matter which way I turn I cannot make myself do right. I want to but I cannot. When I want to do good, I do not; and when I try not to do wrong, I do it anyway.

Now if I am doing what I do not want to, it is plain where the trouble is: sin still has me in its evil grasp.

It seems to be a fact of life that when I want to do what is right, I inevitably do what is wrong. I love to do God's will so far as my new nature is concerned.

But there is something else deep within me, in my lower nature, that is at war with my mind and wins the fight and makes me a slave to the sin that is still within me.

In my mind I want to be God's willing servant but instead I find myself still enslaved to sin.

83

"Do you hear in these words despair? But The Book was not meant to leave you in despair. It was written to tell you that the means to destroy your pride is to dwell on the greatness of God and his Son."

No one anywhere can ever brag in the presence of God.

Be honest in your estimate of yourselves, measuring your value by how much faith God has given you.

Let everyone be sure that he is doing his very best, for then he will have the personal satisfaction of work well done, and will not need to compare himself with someone else. Each of us must bear some faults and burdens of his own. For none of us is perfect!

"The Book will not stoke your dreams of elevating yourselves. This is not a book of phantoms, but The Book of God. And it says to you, 'Reality above all else,' for it comes from the Great Reality who formed it all. And embracing reality, you will see your own failures. And if you lift up your eyes to look beyond them, you will see the grandeur and the mercy of the Holy One. For he says to the fallen and the failing that they are most acceptable when they own up to their deeds and misdeeds. He says to those who bewail their limitations, 'You do not have to be me. Your role as a limited, finite being is acceptable to me.' This begins as the philosophy of dismay, but it becomes the philosophy of triumph."

Then he read to them the words of a finite, failing man who had stepped beyond despair by looking at God.

O Lord, you have examined my heart and know everything about me. You know when I sit or stand. When far away you know my every thought. You chart the path ahead of me, and tell me where to stop and rest.

Every moment, you know where I am. You know

what I am going to say before I even say it. You both pre-
cede and follow me, and place your hand of blessing on
my head.

This is too glorious, too wonderful to believe! I can
never get away from my God! If I go up to heaven, you
are there; if I go down to the place of the dead, you are
there.

How precious it is, Lord, to realize that you are thinking about me constantly! I cannot even count how many
times a day your thoughts turn towards me. And when I
waken in the morning, you are still thinking of me!

Search me, O God, and know my heart; test my
thoughts. Point out anything you find in me that makes
you sad, and lead me along the path of everlasting life.

And there was nothing else to be said about the
self. Though Candice and her friends were bewildered
and annoyed by the Traveler's words, some of the
People of the Valley took comfort, knowing they did
not have to exhaust the costly energy of life in build-
ing themselves up. Martin, who had been young once,
believed now that God was best at being God. In the
blood of this finite man surged not self-loathing, but
joy. And Martin said to himself, "Better to be accepted and embraced by the Divine One than to strive at
being divine."

MONEY
AND
POSSESSIONS

NEAR the square stood the home of a rich trader named Vincent. He had not joined the people gathered in the square because he could observe everything clearly from his balcony.

As Vincent surveyed the scene, he saw all sorts of people. Some of his friends, other rich men, were there. And there were those who had practically no possessions to speak of. Vincent looked down and wondered if this loving Father written about in The Book had indeed made both the rich man and the poor man.

Vincent saw Martin, with whom he had done business in years past. Martin was neither rich nor poor, yet like many of the People of the Valley, Martin had worked hard much of his life. Vincent said to himself, *Did the same God who made me make Martin—and that penniless drifter there on the other side of the square? Or does this God even take notice of who possesses what?*

In a pleasant, businesslike voice, Vincent called down from his balcony to the Unknown Traveler. "You there—what does The Book say about money and homes and clothing and such?" Since Vincent was polite and a proper businessman, he did not wish to sound too inquisitive. But his question was sincere nonetheless.

The Traveler looked toward the man on the balcony. He could see the silk and the gold that Vincent had draped himself with. And he began to read from The Book.

The rich man thinks of his wealth as an impregnable defense, a high wall of safety. What a dreamer!

Rich men are conceited, but their real poverty is evident to the poor.

Like a bird that fills her nest with young she has not hatched and which will soon desert her and fly away, so is the man who gets his wealth by unjust means. Sooner or later he will lose his riches and at the end of his life become a poor old fool.

Jesus said to his disciples, "It is almost impossible for a rich man to get into the Kingdom of Heaven. I say it again—it is easier for a camel to go through the eye of a needle than for a rich man to enter the Kingdom of God!"

"Neither you nor anyone else can serve two masters. You will hate one and show loyalty to the other, or else the other way around—you will be enthusiastic about one and despise the other. You cannot serve both God and money."

Vincent appeared not to be bothered by these words. He absentmindedly ran his forefinger across the lavender silk shirt he wore. The Traveler continued reading.

A rich man had a fertile farm that produced fine crops. In fact, his barns were full to overflowing—he could not get everything in.

He thought about his problem, and finally exclaimed, "I know—I will tear down my barns and build bigger ones! Then I will have room enough. And I will sit back and say to myself, 'Friend, you have enough stored away for years to come. Now take it easy! Wine, women, and song for you!'"

But God said to him, "Fool! Tonight you die. Then who will get it all?"

Yes, every man is a fool who gets rich on earth but not in heaven.

This was not the first time Vincent had heard someone speak this way about wealth. But he knew that most people lived and moved in the realm of envy. So when he heard people speak against wealth, he perceived that they only wanted what he had. Now, listening to the words the Traveler read, he was perplexed, for he realized that the God who made the world and everything in it could not envy a rich man. So he spoke again to the Traveler.

"Say more about this, Traveler. Tell us more about God and why he denies the rich what they have."

The Traveler began to read again from The Book.

Look here, you rich men, now is the time to cry and groan with anguished grief because of all the terrible troubles ahead of you. Your wealth is even now rotting away, and your fine clothes are becoming mere moth-eaten rags.

The value of your gold and silver is dropping fast, yet it will stand as evidence against you, and eat your flesh like fire. That is what you have stored up for yourselves, to receive on that coming day of judgment.

For listen! Hear the cries of the field workers whom you have cheated of their pay. Their cries have reached the ears of the Lord of Hosts.

You have spent your years here on earth having fun, satisfying your every whim, and now your fat hearts are ready for the slaughter. You have condemned and killed good men who had no power to defend themselves against you.

Then Vincent withdrew into his house, not wanting to hear more.

The Traveler knew that the People of the Valley envied Vincent and others like him. When Vincent left the balcony, a vagrant, whose home was the square because he had no other home, watched the elegant curtains on the balcony as they rustled sleepily in the autumn breeze. And for such men as this penniless one the Unknown Traveler read these words from The Book:

Do not be dismayed when evil men grow rich and build their lovely homes. For when they die they carry nothing with them! Their honors will not follow them.

Though a man calls himself happy all through his life—and the world loudly applauds success—yet in the end he dies like everyone else.

All through life their road is smooth! They grow sleek and fat. They are not always in trouble and plagued with problems like everyone else, so their pride sparkles like a jeweled necklace, and their clothing is woven of cruelty!

These fat cats have everything their hearts could ever wish for! They scoff at God and threaten his people. How proudly they speak! They boast against the very heavens, and their words strut through the earth.

God's people are dismayed and confused, and drink it all in. "Does God realize what is going on?" they ask. "Look at these men of arrogance; they never have to lift a finger—theirs is a life of ease; and all the time their riches multiply."

The vagrants in the town square heard these questions from The Book, and they recognized them as questions their own hearts had uttered.

It is so hard to explain it—this prosperity of those who hate the Lord. Then one day I went into God's sanctu-

Did the same God who
made me make Martin—
and that penniless drifter
there on the other side of the square?
Or does this God even take notice
of who possesses what?

ary to meditate, and thought about the future of these
evil men.

What a slippery path they are on—suddenly God will
send them sliding over the edge of the cliff and down to
their destruction: an instant end to all their happiness, an
eternity of terror. Their present life is only a dream! They
will awaken to the truth as one awakens from a dream of
things that never really were!

Do not always be wishing for what you do not have.
For real life and real living are not related to how rich we
are.

It is better to have little and be godly than to own an
evil man's wealth. Better a little with reverence for God,
than great treasure and trouble with it. A little, gained
honestly, is better than great wealth gotten by dishonest
means.

Do not weary yourself trying to get rich. Why waste
your time? For riches can disappear as though they had
the wings of a bird!

The Traveler said to the People of the Valley,
"There are wells reputed to be bottomless. It is said
that you could pour into them forever and ever and
they would not be filled. No one has tried this. But
some have tried to fill themselves, and they have
failed." And he began to read again.

The foolishness of thinking that wealth brings happiness!
He who loves money shall never have enough. The
more you have, the more you spend, right up to the limits
of your income, so what is the advantage of wealth—except perhaps to watch it as it runs through your fingers!
The man who works hard sleeps well whether he eats
little or much, but the rich must worry and suffer in-
somnia.

Do you want to be truly rich? You already are if you
are happy and good. After all, we did not bring any

*money with us when we came into the world, and we
cannot carry away a single penny when we die. So we
should be well satisfied without money if we have enough
food and clothing.*

*But people who long to be rich soon begin to do all
kinds of wrong things to get money, things that hurt them
and make them evil-minded and finally send them to hell
itself.*

*For the love of money is the first step toward all kinds
of sin. Some people have even turned away from God
because of their love for it, and as a result have pierced
themselves with many sorrows.*

Vincent's butler stood on the balcony. He was trou-
bled at these words, for he loved the family he had
served for three decades. Yet he also knew that they
loved their wealth. And he felt led to speak in their
defense, though he could not express himself with
much conviction. He said in a placid voice to the
Traveler, "Your words are harsh, Traveler."

"They are not my words," the Traveler said. "They
are the words of The Book, and The Book is true,
though the truth bites. I would be cruel, and The
Book would not be true, if it only whispered and nuz-
zled." Then he read these words:

*They trust in their wealth and boast about how rich they
are, yet not one of them, though rich as kings, can ran-
som his own brother from the penalty of sin! For God's
forgiveness does not come that way.*

*For a soul is far too precious to be ransomed by mere
earthly wealth. There is not enough of it in all the earth
to buy eternal life for just one soul, to keep it out of hell.*

*Rich man! Proud man! Wise man! You must die like
all the rest!*

*You have no greater lease on life than foolish, stupid
men. You must leave your wealth to others. You name*

your estates after yourselves as though your lands could
be forever yours, and you could live on them eternally.

But man with all his pomp must die like any animal.
Such is the folly of these men, though after they die they
will be quoted as having great wisdom.

Death is the shepherd of all mankind.

Vincent then appeared on his balcony again. He
had been listening to the Traveler inside his house.
Then he spoke again, barely controlling the anger
welling up inside him.

"Sir, we live in a world of foolishness and contra-
dictions. We are told from the cradle on that it is a
grand thing to prosper and have much to show for it.
Then we are told to despise what we have, or to feel
the pains of guilt. Who can do right in such a world?"

"Were you not listening?" the Traveler asked him.
"I read to you the words about a man serving two
masters. What is it that you worship? Worship is what
matters. If you feel guilt biting at your insides, let it
not be guilt over your house or your clothing or the
number of employees you have. Let it be guilt over
gaining by burdening and defrauding others. But even
if you have come by all your wealth honestly, do not
rest too easily. You may feel guilt, and if so, let it be
guilt over the devotion you gave to that frigid idol,
money." He paused, and Vincent waited anxiously for
his next words. "A rich man can be saved. It is hard,
but not impossible. It is not *having*, but *worshiping*
money that keeps rich men from the Kingdom of
God."

Then the Traveler began to read again, and his
words were for both the rich and the poor.

The rich and the poor are alike before the Lord who
made them all. Rich and poor are alike in this: each de-
pends on God for light.

Some he causes to be poor, and others to be rich. For all the earth is the Lord's, and he has set the world in order.

Give me neither poverty nor riches! Give me just enough to satisfy my needs! For if I grow rich, I may become content without God. And if I am too poor, I may steal, and thus insult God's holy name.

A Christian who does not amount to much in this world should be glad, for he is great in the Lord's sight. But a rich man should be glad that his riches mean nothing to the Lord.

My contentment is not in wealth but in seeing God and knowing all is well between us. And when I awake in heaven, I will be fully satisfied, for I will see God face to face.

Seeing the haggard and fretful face of the man who slept in the town square and owned nothing, the Traveler read these words, words from the mouth of the Son of God himself:

Do not worry about things— food, drink, and clothes. For you already have life and a body—and they are far more important than what to eat and wear. Look at the birds! They do not worry about what to eat—they do not need to sow or reap or store up food—for your heavenly Father feeds them.

And you are far more valuable to him than they are. Will all your worries add a single moment to your life?

And why worry about your clothes? Look at the field lilies! They do not worry about theirs. Yet King Solomon in all his glory was not clothed as beautifully as they. And if God cares so wonderfully for flowers that are here today and gone tomorrow, won't he more surely care for you, O men of little faith?

So do not worry at all about having enough food and clothing. Why be like the heathen? For they take pride in

95

all these things and are deeply concerned about them.

But your heavenly Father already knows perfectly well that you need them, and he will give them to you if you give him first place in your life and live as he wants you to.

So do not be anxious about tomorrow. God will take care of your tomorrow too. Live one day at a time.

He read these words because he knew that frail humans often despair in a world where injustice seems to swallow up justice, a world where a small worry can gnaw away the foundations of the surest confidence. Then to strengthen what little faith they had, he read these words:

The Lord says: Let not the wise man bask in his wisdom, nor the mighty man in his might, nor the rich man in his riches.

Let them boast in this alone: That they truly know me, and understand that I am the Lord of justice and of righteousness whose love is steadfast; and that I love to be this way.

"People, know that tonight you sit at your dinner under the eye of the One who knit together every child ever born, whether he was birthed on a bed of silk or in a cattle stall. And if you feast on basted pheasant or on the crumbs that the stray dogs bypass, you and what you eat and what you wear belong to that One." And some wondered if, in God's Kingdom, rich and poor would indeed sit at table together.

GIVING

THE People of the Valley were intrigued by what the Unknown Traveler read to them about money and possessions. Like men and women of every age and every place, they would often neglect matters invisible to their eyes, but they could not forget about the firm material world and the share of it they possessed or wished to possess. The Traveler knew this, and he did not mind, for he knew that God himself had made the material world and took much pleasure in it.

A man named Giles had kinsmen in the Valley, and these were much poorer than he. As he lay in a comfortable bed at night, Giles often wondered if his relations were as comfortable as he was. Yet thoughts of them would vanish like a vapor when Giles told himself, *They deserve what they have, just as I do. It is not my concern.* Yet the thoughts would come back again, like an animal scratching at the door, begging to be let in.

Giles remembered these night thoughts as he stood in the square, watching the russet leaves of the autumn oaks rustling. "It is late in the year," he said to himself, and somehow the waning of the season made him wish to speak to the Traveler.

"Sir, tell us about giving."

The Traveler looked at Giles and noticed that he

resembled another man standing in the square. He could tell these were kin, though except for their faces there was nothing in common between them. Their clothes and their cleanliness were nothing alike. Then the Traveler said, "I cannot speak about giving without speaking about the poor and the help-less. You live in a world of vanity and selfishness, and in such a world the ones in need are those who have no power, no influence, no voice. The penniless man, the woman born with no limbs, the child with an afflicted mind, the baby denied birth, the old couple abandoned by their family—these are the ones you must think of when you think of giving." Then he began to read.

Happy is the generous man, the one who feeds the poor.

If you give to the poor, your needs will be supplied! But a curse upon those who close their eyes to poverty. God blesses those who are kind to the poor. To despise the poor is to sin.

When you help the poor you are lending to the Lord— and he pays wonderful interest on your loan!

Judges must always be just in their sentences, not no-ticing whether a person is poor or rich; they must always be perfectly fair.

Give fair judgment to the poor man, the afflicted, the fatherless, the destitute. Rescue the poor and helpless from the grasp of evil men.

Tell those who are rich not to be proud and not to trust in their money. Tell them to use their money to do good. They should be rich in good works and should give happily to those in need, always being ready to share with others whatever God has given them.

By doing this they will be storing up real treasure for themselves in heaven—it is the only safe investment for eternity! And they will be living a fruitful life down here as well.

The good man knows the poor man's rights; the godless do not care.

Stop oppressing those who work for you. Treat them fairly and give them what they earn. I want you to share your food with the hungry and bring right into your own homes those who are helpless, poor and destitute. Clothe those who are cold and do not hide from relatives who need your help.

Give to those who ask, and do not turn away from those who want to borrow.

Do not forget about those in jail. Suffer with them as though you were there yourself. Share the sorrow of those being mistreated, for you know what they are going through.

If you give even a cup of cold water to a little child, you will surely be rewarded.

If you do these things, God will shed his own glorious light upon you. He will heal you; your godliness will lead you forward, and goodness will be a shield before you, and the glory of the Lord will protect you from behind.

Martin was listening closely. He believed these words were directed to the rich people there. Yet he knew he himself had enough to share at least something with those who had less. So now he addressed the Traveler. "Sir, can you give us rules or guidelines for giving?"

The Traveler looked with compassion on this man, the first of the Valley's inhabitants he had encountered. He understood Martin's heart, though he had met him only recently. He knew Martin was a comfortable man, yet an uncomfortable man, a man with questions, a searching man. And he knew that searching people often feel desperate, and that desperation yearns for quick solutions and tidy formulas. So the Traveler asked him, "Do you know the meaning of 'tithe,' Martin?"

99

Martin replied, "It means a tenth part—ten percent. Is that what we are required to give?"

The Traveler understood clearly how such words as *require* and *percentage* could well mean the end of genuine giving and compassion. So he read to the people these words:

On every Lord's Day each of you should put aside something from what you have earned during the week, and use it for this offering. The amount depends on how much the Lord has helped you earn.

If you are really eager to give, then it is not important how much you have to give. God wants you to give what you have, not what you do not have.

But remember this—if you give little, you will get little. A farmer who plants just a few seeds will get only a small crop, but if he plants much, he will reap much.

Everyone must make up his own mind as to how much he should give. Do not force anyone to give more than he really wants to, for cheerful givers are the ones God prizes.

God is able to make it up to you by giving you everything you need and more, so that there will not only be enough for your own needs, but plenty left over to give joyfully to others.

The godly man gives generously to the poor. His good deeds will be an honor to him forever.

If you give, you will get! Your gift will return to you in full and overflowing measure, pressed down, shaken together to make room for more, and running over. Whatever measure you use to give—large or small—will be used to measure what is given back to you.

When he had read these words, the Traveler said, "Did you not know that any act of kindness you do is done for the Son of God himself?"

A young woman asked, "How can that be? We know that the Son of God once walked the earth as a man of flesh and blood. But he is not here now."

Pleased at the woman's attentiveness, the Traveler then read this parable told by the Son of God, who was speaking of the judgment that would take place at the end of the world:

When I, the Messiah, shall come in my glory, I will separate the people as a shepherd separates the sheep from the goats, and place the sheep at my right hand, and the goats at my left.

Then I, the King, shall say to those at my right, "Come, blessed into the Kingdom prepared for you. For I was hungry and you fed me; I was thirsty and you gave me water; I was a stranger and you invited me into your homes; naked and you clothed me; sick and in prison, and you visited me."

Then these righteous ones will reply, "Sir, when did we ever see you hungry and feed you? Or thirsty and give you anything to drink? Or a stranger, and help you? Or naked, and clothe you? When did we ever see you sick or in prison, and visit you?"

And I will tell them, "When you did it to these my brothers you were doing it to me!" Then I will turn to those on my left and say, "Away with you, you cursed ones, into the eternal fire. For I was hungry and you would not feed me; thirsty, and you would not give me anything to drink; a stranger, and you refused me hospitality; naked, and you would not clothe me; sick, and in prison, and you did not visit me."

Then they will reply, "Lord, when did we ever see you hungry or thirsty or a stranger or naked or sick or in prison, and not help you?"

And I will answer, "When you refused to help the least of these my brothers, you were refusing help to me."

A woman named Lila was considered by her friends to be a devout woman, a woman who understood the things of the soul. She asked the Traveler, "Sir, is it not true that God cares more for our spiritual needs than our material needs? Should we not seek more for what is eternal than for what passes away?"

These words were not new to the ears of the Traveler. While walking the roads of a selfish world he had seen that men and women often cover up their callousness with eloquent excuses. For such as these the Traveler read these words from The Book:

If you have a friend who is in need of food and clothing, and you say to him, "Well, good-bye and God bless you; stay warm and eat hearty," and then do not give him clothes or food, what good does that do?

If someone has money enough to live well, and sees a brother in need, and will not help him—how can God's love be within him?

Little children, let us stop just saying we love people; let us really love them, and show it by our actions. Then we will know for sure, by our actions, that we are on God's side, and our consciences will be clear, even when we stand before the Lord.

A very wealthy man was there, and his face beamed as he listened to these words. While the Traveler was reading, this man glanced around him and noticed some people looking at him with approval. And he was pleased, for he had given freely to charities of various kinds. He was regarded by all who knew him as a magnanimous giver, though he was often bothered by the Valley's vagrants passing through his property. He cleared his throat and said to the Traveler, "Well spoken, every word of it. What you have said I say to all my friends. We who have much must give much."

The Traveler could discern the man's assurance and self-satisfaction. He began to read again from The Book.

Take care! Do not do your good deeds publicly, to be admired, for then you will lose the reward from your Father in heaven.

When you give a gift to a beggar, do not shout about it as the hypocrites do—blowing trumpets in the streets to call attention to their acts of charity! I tell you in all earnestness, they have received all the reward they will ever get.

But when you do a kindness to someone, do it secretly—do not tell your left hand what your right hand is doing. And your Father who knows all secrets will reward you.

When the Traveler spoke these words, the wealthy man withdrew from the square. He was a busy man, and he had heard enough for one day.

Martin saw him walking away, and he said to the Traveler, "What you have read makes sense. You are saying that motivation is what matters. What is righteous is not the deed of kindness itself, but the chaste heart from which the deed issues."

The Traveler nodded in approval, then read them this story of the Son of God's meeting with a man whose heart became chaste:

As Jesus was passing through Jericho, a man named Zacchaeus, one of the most influential Jews in the Roman tax-collecting business (and, of course, a very rich man), tried to get a look at Jesus, but he was too short to see over the crowds. So he ran ahead and climbed into a sycamore tree beside the road, to watch from there.

When Jesus came by he looked up at Zacchaeus and

called him by name! "Zacchaeus! Quick! Come down! I am going to be a guest in your home today!"

Zacchaeus hurriedly climbed down and took Jesus to his house in great excitement and joy.

But the crowds were displeased. "He has gone to be the guest of a notorious sinner," they grumbled.

Meanwhile, Zacchaeus stood before the Lord and said, "Sir, from now on I will give half my wealth to the poor, and if I find I have overcharged anyone on his taxes, I will penalize myself by giving him back four times as much!"

Jesus told him, "This shows that salvation has come to this home today. I have come to search for and to save such souls as his."

And when Martin heard this, he smiled, and it was the smile of one whose heart and mind has been stretched by the truth. The Unknown Traveler was pleased to see his joy, for it was for this that he had come to the Valley.

WORK
AND
PLAY

A MAN with callused hands stood among the people. His name was Marcus, and he had toiled many years. His father and his father's father had taught him that work was the chief end of life. And he had believed this, though his heart often filled up with bitterness, angry that his days had seemed nothing more than a mingling of sweat and weariness and small gains.

Marcus could see among the people the man he had labored under for many years. When he looked at this man's fair skin, the fine texture of his hands, and the neatness of his clothes, Marcus clenched his fists. Then he thought of his father and his words about the dignity of labor. And he wondered if the Traveler had anything to tell the people about work.

Marcus's employer, who always spoke with measured dignity, addressed the Traveler, hoping the Traveler would speak words to encourage the workers' diligence.

"Sir, does The Book have anything to tell these people about the value of hard work?"

The Unknown Traveler understood this man and his purpose, yet he spoke these words from The Book, words which at first satisfied the employer:

Hard work means prosperity; only a fool idles away his time.

Work hard and become a leader; be lazy and never succeed.

A lazy man will not even dress the game he gets while hunting, but the diligent man makes good use of everything he finds.

Lazy people want much but get little, while the diligent are prospering.

An empty stable stays clean—but there is no income from an empty stable.

The Traveler was holding The Book high. Then he began to speak again, knowing that Marcus and people like him were present.

"Does it pain some of you to lift up your heads to see this? Are some of you so weary from your labor that your backs and necks are bent? Listen to the words of one who questioned the value of work."

I found great pleasure in hard work. This pleasure was, indeed, my only reward for all my labors.

But as I looked at everything I had tried, it was all so useless, a chasing of the wind, and there was nothing really worthwhile anywhere. And I am disgusted about this, that I must leave the fruits of all my hard work to others. How discouraging!

So I turned in despair from hard work as the answer to my search for satisfaction. For though I spend my life searching for wisdom, knowledge, and skill, I must leave all of it to someone who has not done a day's work in his life; he inherits all my efforts, free of charge. This is not only foolish, but unfair.

So what does a man get for all his hard work? Days full of sorrow and grief, and restless, bitter nights. It is all utterly ridiculous.

How frail is man, how few his days, how full of trouble! He blossoms for a moment like a flower.

"True, true!" It was Marcus who spoke, and words did not come easily to Marcus. "So what is the point of it all, then? We break our backs, and someone else benefits."

The Traveler had compassion on this man. He smiled a smile of understanding and pity, and Marcus's angry look melted somewhat. Then the Traveler spoke these words from The Book:

The Lord God placed the man in the Garden of Eden as its gardener, to tend and care for it.

"You see, my friend," said the Traveler, "from the very beginning you have had this mandate. You must work. God the Creator worked to form this universe, and he still works to sustain it. Yet he cares for you who labor. He himself rested from his work, and he commands rest for his creatures."

Remember to observe the Sabbath as a holy day. Six days a week are for your daily duties and your regular work, but the seventh day is a day of Sabbath rest before the Lord your God.
On that day you are to do no work of any kind. For in six days the Lord made the heaven, earth, and sea, and everything in them, and rested the seventh day; so he blessed the Sabbath day and set it aside for rest.

"The loving Father who made this weary world and blesses it with good things desires your love and worship. You are to worship him alone, not your work, and not the things you gain from your labor. O people, how many of you worship your work, expecting it to satisfy every want of your eye and your heart, and it was not meant to do that. Do you not understand that work and worship are not the same? Do you not see

107

that work for its own sake is folly? Work because you must—you have heard the words from The Book. But take pleasure in your rest also, as The Book tells you." Then the Traveler read these words from The Book:

One thing, at least, is good: It is for a man to eat well, drink a good glass of wine, accept his position in life, and enjoy his work whatever his job may be, for however long the Lord may let him live.

To enjoy your work and to accept your lot in life— that is indeed a gift from God. The person who does that will not need to look back with sorrow on his past, for God gives him joy.

Never be lazy in your work but serve the Lord enthusiastically. This should be your ambition: to live a quiet life, minding your own business and doing your own work.

As a result, people will trust and respect you, and you will not need to depend on others for enough money to pay your bills.

Some of the younger men and women were listening critically, for they did not highly value work, and they knew that for them work was not essential. They lived only for pleasure, and for them every day was a day of rest, though not set aside for worshiping the Lord. Day in and day out, all was an endless round of jollity. And they knew that some of the people who labored hard also envied them. For these people so obsessed with pleasure, the Traveler said these words from The Book:

I said to myself, "Come now, be merry; enjoy yourself to the full." But I found that this, too, was futile. For it is silly to be laughing all the time; what good does it do?

So, after a lot of thinking, I decided to try the road of drink. Next I changed my course again and followed the path of folly, so that I could experience the only happiness most men have throughout their lives.

Next I bought slaves, both men and women, and others were born within my household. I also bred great herds and flocks, more than any of the kings before me. I collected silver and gold as taxes from many kings and provinces. In the cultural arts, I organized men's and women's choirs and orchestras.

Anything I wanted, I took, and did not restrain myself from any joy.

But as I looked at everything I had tried, it was all so useless, a chasing of the wind, and there was nothing really worthwhile anywhere.

When the Unknown Traveler said these words, some of the young people laughed to themselves. But a few were touched inwardly, for they knew that they, like the one whose words were recorded in The Book, found that pleasure for its own sake was vain and trifling.

The Traveler then spoke further on this.

Woe to you who get up early in the morning to go on long drinking bouts that last till late at night. You furnish lovely music at your grand parties; the orchestras are superb! But for the Lord you have no thought or care.

You sing and dance and play, and feast and drink. "Let us eat, drink, and be merry," you say. "What's the difference, for tomorrow we die."

"People of the Valley," the Traveler said, closing The Book for a moment, "do not believe for a moment that the God who spangled the sky with multicolored birds and dappled the fields with wildflowers would deny you joy and play. Consider the words of God's Son himself."

My purpose is to give life in all its fullness. I have told you this so that you will be filled with my joy. Yes, your cup of joy will overflow.

Then the Traveler broke into a radiant smile, and his joy beamed over the square and the people gathered there. His voice was jubilant as he read these words:

Rejoice in your Maker. O people, exult in your King. Praise his name with dancing, accompanied by drums and lyre.

Rejoice before the Lord your God in everything you do.

Happy are all who search for God, and always do his will.

The words the Traveler had read settled like weights in the hearts and minds of the People of the Valley. But as they pondered them, a flock of brightly colored finches flew over the square, whistling and chattering like a pack of children let out of school. And the People of the Valley could see that the Maker of the universe took delight in his creatures' frolics.

THE BODY

*T*HE hollow eyes and the pallor of some who had wasted themselves showed on the faces of some who were there watching the Unknown Traveler. Among these was a man named Owen, who was only thirty years old, though the lines in his face added another ten years to his look. Owen was not drunk, though he had been the night before. He was glad when clouds covered the sun that day, for bright sunlight stung his eyes.

Some who had wasted themselves were not pale, and their eyes were bright. Yet inwardly—and the wise, somewhat like God, see inwardly—these were ugly. For ugliness lies in not being what the Maker of both matter and spirit destined things to be.

The woman Owen lived with was not there. She was at their dwelling, and Owen hoped she was alone, though he knew this was unlikely. But he was not sure this mattered, for she was not his first woman, and he did not expect her to be his last.

This man had enjoyed his youth to the full, and though he could not ignore the changed face in his mirror, he was unwilling to change the pursuits of his youth. His body, he knew, was not as lean or tight or desirable as it once had been, yet he still perceived it as something to be spent in nothing more than pleasure. And this was how he perceived others. He never lacked for companions who saw the world as he saw it.

But on this particular day his flesh called out for nothing more than a respite. His head and stomach throbbed, one seeming full and the other empty, and what seemed like a fever washed over him every few moments. And so he was in the square, away from his woman and away from the tavern, somehow feeling drawn to this Unknown Traveler and The Book that had been so long forgotten.

A cloud passed over, and Owen's eyes felt some relief at having the sun obscured for a time. The Traveler began to speak to the People of the Valley.

"There is not one blade of grass, there is no color in this world that is not intended to make us rejoice. We are put into this world not only to be spectators in this beautiful theatre, but to enjoy the vast bounty and variety of good things which are offered to us in it. You have eyes and ears and your other senses because the Creator made this infinite variety for his pleasure, and for yours. Yet because selfishness and vanity mar every bit of creation, this flesh you are made of is subject to all kinds of abuses."

Then the Traveler began to read to them from The Book.

When you follow your own wrong inclinations your lives will produce these evil results: impure thoughts, eagerness for lustful pleasure, idolatry, spiritism (that is, encouraging the activity of demons), hatred and fighting, jealousy and anger, constant effort to get the best for yourself, complaints and criticisms, the feeling that everyone else is wrong, wrong doctrine, envy, murder, drunkenness, wild parties, and all that sort of thing.

You drink wine by the bucketful, caring nothing at all that your brothers need your help. Wine gives false cour-

age, hard liquor leads to brawls. What fools men are to let it master them, making them reel drunkenly down the street.

The people commit adultery wholesale and gang up at the city's brothels. They are well-fed, lusty stallions, each neighing for his neighbor's mate.

Lust is a shameful sin, a crime that should be punished. It is a devastating fire that destroys to hell.

You can be sure of this: The Kingdom of God will never belong to anyone who is impure or greedy, for a greedy person is really an idol worshiper—he loves and worships the good things of this life more than God. Those who live immoral lives, who are idol worshipers, adulterers, or homosexuals, will have no share in his Kingdom. Neither will thieves or greedy people, drunkards, slanderers, or robbers.

Do not be fooled by those who try to excuse these sins, for the terrible wrath of God is upon all those who do them.

Owen had opened his mouth to speak, but his mind was fogged, and he had no vigor left in him after the previous night. The Traveler continued to read.

You know how late it is; time is running out. Wake up, for the coming of the Lord is nearer now than when we first believed. The night is far gone, the day of his return will soon be here.

So quit the evil deeds of darkness and put on the armor of right living, as we who live in the daylight should! Be decent and true in everything you do so that all can approve your behavior. Do not spend your time in wild parties and getting drunk or in adultery and lust, or fighting, or jealousy. And do not make plans to enjoy evil.

Follow the steps of the godly instead, and stay on the

right path, for only good men enjoy life to the full; evil men lose the good things they might have had, and they themselves shall be destroyed.

Live no longer as the unsaved do, for they are blinded and confused. Their closed hearts are full of darkness. They are far away from the life of God because they have shut their minds against him, and they cannot understand his ways. They do not care anymore about right and wrong and have given themselves over to impure ways. They stop at nothing, being driven by their evil minds and reckless lusts.

But that is not the way Christ taught you! If you have really heard his voice and learned from him the truths concerning himself, then throw off your old evil nature—the old you that was a partner in your evil ways—rotten through and through, full of lust and sham.

Now your attitudes and thoughts must all be constantly changing for the better. Yes, you must be a new and different person, holy and good. Clothe yourself with this new nature.

Sexual sin is never right: our bodies were not made for that, but for the Lord, and the Lord wants to fill our bodies with himself. No other sin affects the body as this one does. When you sin this sin it is against your own body.

Do not drink too much wine, for many evils lie along that path; be filled instead with the Holy Spirit, and controlled by him.

Have you not yet learned that your body is the home of the Holy Spirit God gave you, and that he lives within you? Your own body does not belong to you. For God has bought you with a great price. So use every part of your body to give glory back to God, because he owns it.

Though once your heart was full of darkness, now it is full of light from the Lord, and your behavior should show it! Because of this light within you, you should do only what is good and right and true.

A certain woman, who had lived a very clean and sober life, was nodding her head in agreement. She said to the Traveler, "How true this all is. Throughout my life I have watched my companions and my children's companions wasting themselves away. The flesh—that is what pollutes our lives."

But the Traveler shook his head, knowing how humans liked to blame their failings on external things. He began to read again.

It is the thought-life that pollutes. For from within, out of men's hearts, come evil thoughts of lust, theft, murder, adultery, wanting what belongs to others, wickedness, deceit, lewdness, envy, slander, pride, and all other folly. All these vile things come from within; they are what pollute you and make you unfit for God.

There was a time when some of you were just like that, but now your sins are washed away, and you are set apart for God, and he has accepted you because of what the Lord Jesus Christ and the Spirit of our God have done for you.

Owen found his voice, and he said to the Traveler, "What The Book tells us is that our life is not only to be without sin, but without joy. Does God not give us rules to drain all the color out of life? My friends would laugh at me for leading such a life, and they would be right to do so."

The Unknown Traveler said, "No color of the spectrum is denied to those who love God. Pity it is that so many of you assume that the God of heaven despises pleasure and frames rules so that men and women will offend him if they smile. Would he who designed every part of you forbid you to feel joy in it? Listen to the words of a man who poured out poetry because his desire had set his mind on fire."

I am here in my garden, my darling, my bride! I gather my myrrh with my spices and eat my honeycomb with my honey. I drink my wine.

How sweet is your love, my darling, my bride. How much better it is than mere wine. The perfume of your love is more fragrant than all the richest spices. Your lips, my dear, are made of honey. You dance so beautifully.

Kiss me again and again, for your love is sweeter than wine. Oh, feed me with your love, for I am utterly love-sick.

Oh, lover and beloved, eat and drink! Yes, drink deeply!

"These words are from The Book of the Lord. Do you still believe he wants you to close your eyes to this world's pleasures? It is not pleasure that the Almighty despises—it is the abuse of pleasure, worshiping it, pursuing it to the sad neglect of duty and honor. The same hands that rightly caress your husbands and wives, and raise a hearty glass at family feasts—these hands were made for other things as well. Let the same hand that burned like fire on the wedding night also bandage the wounds of a friend, lift a fallen one from the gutter, and wipe a tear from a prisoner's face."

And the Traveler began to read again.

When the Holy Spirit controls our lives he will produce this kind of fruit in us: love, joy, peace, patience, kindness, goodness, faithfulness, gentleness and self-control.

You have had enough in the past of the evil things the godless enjoy—sex sin, lust, getting drunk, wild parties, drinking bouts, and the worship of idols, and other terrible sins.

Of course, your former friends will be very surprised when you do not eagerly join them any more in the wick-

*ed things they do, and they will laugh at you in contempt
and scorn. But just remember that they must face the
Judge of all, living and dead; they will be punished for the
way they have lived.*

*Our homeland is in heaven, where our Savior the
Lord Jesus Christ is; and we are looking forward to his
return from there. When he comes back he will take
these dying bodies of ours and change them into glorious
bodies like his own.*

Owen pondered these things for a moment. And
while he was thinking, one of his drinking companions spoke up. "What kind of God is it that The Book
gives witness to? Is he a God only of rules and restric-
tions? Would a loving God take pleasure in seeing his
loved ones tangled up in a web of endless regulations?
What about freedom? Must the pleasures of our
bodies be bounded, pressed into proper channels?
Why can we not do whatever we please, so long as we
do not abuse someone?"

The Traveler said, "It is true that rules are not the
essence of right living. If the heart of God had win-
dows, you would look inside and not see laws and
rules, but love. Yet fathers do make rules, because
their children are frail and lack understanding. And
God is a father, and he knows your weaknesses, and
he knows how easily you slip into bondage to what
you think you control."

Then the Traveler read these words from the pen of
one who had understood both law and love:

*I can do anything I want to if Christ has not said no, but
some of these things are not good for me. Even if I am
allowed to do them, I will refuse to if I think they might
get such a grip on me that I cannot easily stop when I
want to.*

117

Take the matter of eating. God has given us an appetite for food and stomachs to digest it. But that does not mean we should eat more than we need. Do not think of eating as important, because some day God will do away with both stomachs and food.

The pallid young man Owen walked away from the square, not in anger at the Traveler or The Book, but at his own flesh that seemed embittered against him. And while his throbbing head murmured to him his need for change in his life, the power of habit tugged him homeward, drawing him back into a wearisome cycle of satisfaction and regret.

But Owen's companion stayed to hear more, for no one had ever spoken before about how God, dwelling as the Holy Spirit within a man, could bring about transformation.

Seeing that the People of the Valley yearned for words of comfort, the Traveler read these words:

Fix your thoughts on what is true and good and right. Whatever is good and perfect comes to us from God, the Creator of all light. Think about things that are pure and lovely, and dwell on the fine, good things in others.

A person who is pure of heart sees goodness and purity in everything. Think about all you can praise God for and be glad about.

Give your bodies to God. Let them be a living sacrifice, holy—the kind he can accept. When you think of what he has done for you, is this too much to ask?

Do not copy the behavior and customs of this world, but be a new and different person with a fresh newness in all you do and think. Then you will learn from your own experience how his ways will really satisfy you.

Let us turn away from everything wrong, whether of body or spirit, and purify ourselves, living in the wholesome fear of God, giving ourselves to him alone.

A man in mid-life, a man who knew the world's patterns, was listening. He had changed much in recent years. He was not angry or guilty over his past, but he was a faithful student of it. After many years he had learned to politely decline the things that once seemed irresistible. And his family rejoiced, and he rejoiced. He said to the Traveler, "Once God signs his name across a man's heart, the signature burns through to every particle of him. His days of living for only himself are doomed, and every grain of him is marked for God. And he will sleep well at night only when he makes good on his dedication. When body and soul join in one grand effort for the Lord, the man will sleep the sleep of the just." And many who knew the man well nodded their agreement.

Then the Traveler dismissed them all, for it was the middle of the day. And he asked them to go to their homes, and to eat and drink and be glad that the Maker of heaven and earth had given them their senses. Within himself he prayed that they would ponder the words they had just heard and remember that they need not be mere slaves to their desires.

JUSTICE
AND
LAW

T HE VALLEY had its laws
and those who served to carry out the laws. And the
Valley was no different from any other place, for in it
were some people who hated laws because they despised all authority. Yet some hated the laws because
justice was not easily had. And abuse of justice, like
storm and fire and untimely death, is no less painful
because it is inevitable.

Throughout the centuries, spattered as they are
with innocent blood, the philosophers and the prophets have puzzled over man's chafing at what is un-
avoidable. They have asked why a people prone to
falseness and evil would shed tears at what they and
their kindred brought into being. And the philosophers reach no conclusions, though some say that
people remember a time when no falseness marred
the face of earth. And some say that what acts in the
brain made feverish by injustice is not remembrance,
but vision, the vision of a time or place when the
inequities will be planed away. The arguments continue, and the yoke of falseness still weighs upon the
neck of humanity.

Of those who returned to the square that afternoon
were some who carried out the laws. And far from
them, though listening with no less interest to the

Unknown Traveler's words, were those who had been wounded by the laws. And some of these had been wounded justly, for it is in the scheme of things that true criminals do sometimes receive what they deserve. But some of the wounded ones were victims, for victims are found in every place. Even where sacrifices are not burned on altars, sacrifices there are.

Lara, a woman whose husband was in prison, was thinking of the God of heaven. She was considering whether the lofty One, the One who formed the elements and the laws that govern them, took note of the endless round of making rules, breaking rules, subverting rules, perverting justice—until the innocent and the gullible despaired of truth ever raising its gasping head above the flood of falsehood.

And Lara, whose voice was hard, though it had not always been so, spoke to the Traveler.

"Speak to us of justice—if The Book has anything to say about it."

Then the Traveler began to read these words to show them that equity was never far from the heart of God:

The Lord despises those who say that bad is good, and good is bad.

The Traveler knew that these would be hollow words for some, so he read these words to assure the people that God indeed took note of soured justice:

Woe to those who drag their sins behind them like a bullock on a rope. They even mock the Holy One and dare the Lord to punish them.

"Hurry up and punish us, O Lord," they say. "We want to see what you can do!" They say that what is right is wrong, and what is wrong is right; that black is

white and white is black; bitter is sweet and sweet is bitter.

Perceiving that these words pinched the people's minds, the Traveler continued.

Throughout the earth justice is giving way to crime, and even the police courts are corrupt.

Truth is gone, and anyone who tries a better life is soon attacked.

Yes, we know what sinners we are. We know our disobedience; we have denied the Lord our God. We know what rebels we are and how unfair we are, for we carefully plan our lies. Our courts oppose the righteous man; fairness is unknown. Truth falls dead in the streets, and justice is outlawed.

You have trampled and crushed beneath your feet the lowly of the world, and deprived men of their God-given rights, and refused them justice.

Evil men, you make "justice" a bitter pill for the poor and oppressed. "Righteousness" and "fair play" are meaningless fictions to you!

How you hate honest judges! How you despise people who tell the truth! You trample the poor and steal their smallest crumb by all your taxes, fines, and usury.

You are the enemies of everything good. You take bribes. You refuse justice to the poor.

You go at your evil deeds with both hands, and how skilled you are in using them! The governor and judge alike demand bribes. The rich man pays them off and tells them whom to ruin. Justice is twisted between them.

Then the Traveler gazed into the severe face of Lara. Her eyes were blue, but not a youthful blue, the blue of flowers and summer horizons and gemstones. Hers were a faded, pained blue, like old linen grown rawer and rougher from too much washing.

Lara stood next to her friend, a woman her own age, a friend whose eyes were not hard but compassionate. And the Traveler spoke these words, for they gave expression to her friend's voiceless eyes:

Must I forever see this sin and sadness all around me?
Wherever I look there is oppression and bribery and men who love to argue and to fight. The law is not enforced and there is no justice given in the courts, for the wicked far outnumber the righteous, and bribes and trickery prevail.

"People of the Valley," the Traveler said, "the God of heaven and all who honor him know that this fragmented world's laws are only shadows of laws more binding and more enduring. Every law, and every maker of laws, answers not to the petty written rules that change from one city to another. All must answer to a higher law, and to the One who ordered the world and everything in it."

It is wrong to sentence the poor and let the rich go free. He who says to the wicked, "You are innocent," shall be cursed, but blessings shall be showered on those who rebuke sin fearlessly. It is wrong for a judge to favor the wicked and condemn the innocent.
Giving preferred treatment to rich people is a clear case of selling one's soul for a piece of bread. A man's poverty is no excuse for twisting justice against him. Judges must always be just in their sentences, not noticing whether a person is poor or rich; they must always be perfectly fair.
Take no bribes, for a bribe makes you unaware of what you clearly see! A bribe hurts the cause of the person who is right.

*Do not oppress foreigners; you know what it is like to
be a foreigner.*

*You must not curse the deaf nor trip up a blind man
as he walks.*

*You shall not rob nor oppress anyone, and you shall
pay your hired workers promptly. If something is due
them, do not even keep it overnight.*

*Give fair judgment to the poor man, the afflicted, the
fatherless, the destitute. Rescue the poor and helpless
from the grasp of evil men.*

The friend of Lara knew that there could never be
justice in the land unless the people pursued the truth
with a passion. And then the Traveler read these
words about the truth:

*Keep far away from falsely charging anyone with evil.
Never let an innocent person be put to death. I will not
stand for this.*

*When on the witness stand, do not be swayed in your
testimony by the mood of the majority present, and do
not slant your testimony in favor of a man just because
he is poor.*

*Do not pass along untrue reports. Do not cooperate
with an evil man by affirming on the witness stand something you know is false.*

Some of the People of the Valley took heart at
these words, but others scoffed to themselves, for they
knew that every rule, whether from God or man,
would be trampled in the mud in the name of selfishness. And for the scoffers, who understood a portion
of the truth, the Traveler read these words:

*If you see some poor man being oppressed by the rich,
with miscarriage of justice anywhere throughout the land,*

do not be surprised! For every official is under orders from higher up, and the higher officials look up to their superiors. And so the matter is lost in red tape and bureaucracy.

"Dear people, those who oppress and who are oppressed, never cease to believe in the just One who rules. And never cease to pray for the ones bearing the burden for meting out justice. You curse them, and you covet their power and their gains, but neither is right. You end by wallowing in your spite and envy. Pray for them, asking your Creator to lessen the weight of injustice on the victims." And he read them this prayer:

O God, help the ruler to judge as you would. Help him to give justice to your people, even to the poor. May the mountains and hills flourish in prosperity because of his good reign. Help him to defend the poor and needy and to crush their oppressors.

May the poor and needy revere you constantly, as long as sun and moon continue in the skies! Yes, forever!

Standing against a pillar in the square were two brothers, hardly out of their boyhood. And they were full of malice, for they saw before them daily the workings of inequity, yet they could not see the God of heaven, and they doubted his concern for justice. Often the anger that only youth can feel pricked their insides like a holly's thorns. And when the Traveler spoke of praying for the keepers of the law, one of the brothers laughed.

"What do we owe the ones whose rules break our backs? There are others who could bring more fairness to the Valley." And he spoke loudly, hoping the officials would see him and take note. Hatred, when it is on fire, sheds its anonymity.

126

What do we owe the ones
    whose rules break our backs?
There are others who
    could bring more fairness
        to the Valley.

SECRETS FROM THE BOOK

The Traveler, knowing that youth and those with the minds of youth despise all authority but themselves, read them this story of the Son of God:

The Pharisees met together to try to think of some way to trap Jesus into saying something for which they could arrest him. They decided to send some of their men along with the Herodians to ask him this question: "Sir, we know you are very honest and teach the truth regardless of the consequences, without fear or favor. Now tell us, is it right to pay taxes to the Roman government or not?"

But Jesus saw what they were after. "You hypocrites!" he exclaimed. "Who are you trying to fool with your trick questions? Here, show me a coin." And they handed him a penny.

"Whose picture is stamped on it?" he asked them. "And whose name is this beneath the picture?"

"Caesar's," they replied.

"Well, then," he said, "give it to Caesar if it is his, and give God everything that belongs to God."

"Do you think," the Traveler asked, "that this Caesar, this emperor of the world, received unbroken praise from all his subjects? Do you not know that the peace laid upon the land by the callous and insolent Romans was bought at the cost of a hundred rivers of blood and a measureless expense of a nation's dignity? Like every king who ever had a knee bowed to him, this emperor committed both good and bad, and how well the Son of God must have known that this was so." Then the Traveler read these words:

Obey the government, for God is the one who has put it there. There is no government anywhere that God has not placed in power. Those who refuse to obey the laws of the land are refusing to obey God, and punishment will follow.

Pay your taxes, too. For government workers need to be paid so that they can keep on doing God's work, serving you. Pay everyone whatever he ought to have: pay your taxes and import duties gladly, obey those over you, and give honor and respect to all those to whom it is due.

You are free from the law, but that does not mean you are free to do wrong. Live as those who are free to do only God's will at all times.

Show respect for everyone. Fear God and honor the government.

At hearing this, the two angry brothers walked away. For they could not then believe that the God spoken of in The Book truly cared for the poor and the downtrodden.

And some of the other people there, both young and not young, were with them in spirit. Raw youth possess the vigor for revolt, but so often they are cheered on by their staid elders, who remember well their own earlier rebellion and how noble it feels to yell and hurl mud at fattened, lazy officials. So some elders took pleasure in seeing the two brothers like young leopards clawing the turf, wailing for prey.

But some people took the Traveler's words to heart. Martin did, though part of him doubted that Almighty God intended men to obey evil rulers and not question them. So Martin spoke for himself and for others and said to the Traveler, "Is it ever right and proper to disobey? We understand that the One who ordered everything, even order itself, wishes to keep us from the fear and despair of anarchy. And we know it is right to obey the laws and to pray for those who make them. But is it always possible? When the Son of God also told us to give God what belongs to God, surely he knew that doing one may hinder us from the other."

The Traveler said, "Dear people, Jesus, the Son of God, while he walked this earth, used his power to heal many people. After he departed this world, his followers did many of the same miracles, as he told them they would. And for proclaiming God's truth to the people, the people who had for centuries awaited the Son of God's coming, the two men were jailed. And the people's Council, the very ones who should have welcomed the Son of God and his followers, brought them to trial." Then the Traveler read these words:

Peter and John replied, "You decide whether God wants us to obey you instead of him! We cannot stop telling about the wonderful things we saw Jesus do and heard him say."

And Martin understood more than he had before. But he and all the people there were still perplexed, for they despaired over real justice ever reigning on the earth. And so the Traveler gave them assurance, for he could taste their anguish in the autumn air.

In due season God will judge everything man does, both good and bad.
God stands up to open heaven's court. He pronounces judgment on the judges.

"People, you will never see true justice in this world. You may have the vision of it—indeed, you must have that vision always burning within you—but you will not see it brought to pass. It cannot be so. This world's journal is a long and tedious tale of one king followed by another, one more just than the next, the other a little less so, then a dynasty toppled by another, judging the cruelties of the first, yet engendering its own. A crown and a scepter are buried, and the one who wore them is cursed, but the new commander makes a crown for himself, and others envy him, and they wait their chance, and the pitiful tale goes on. But do not believe that only the poor are afflicted in this tale. Rich and poor alike suffer, oppressors and oppressed are wounded, injustice blights both the abased and their governors. No one who draws breath is untouched. And those who plot one revolution after another only fool themselves for a time. And while you struggle against the wrong, do not believe you will ever root it out. It is stronger than you. Yet believe in this One who will bring the right to the fore." Then the Traveler read sobering words to the People of the Valley.

Dear brothers, you are only visitors here. Your real home is in heaven.

Here is your part: Tell the truth. Be fair. Live at peace with everyone.

Happy are those who long to be just and good, for they shall be completely satisfied. Happy are the kind and merciful, for they shall be shown mercy. Happy are those whose hearts are pure, for they shall see God. Happy are those who strive for peace—they shall be called the sons of God. Happy are those who are persecuted because they are good, for the Kingdom of Heaven is theirs.

Lara, the woman whose husband was in prison, raised up her eyes to heaven and prayed that the Lord, the Judge of all the earth, would pour out his peace upon every victim. And Martin, who knew her, and who bled inside for her, prayed also for those who practice injustice. He prayed that they would remember those they had abused. He longed for them to recall the One whose just rule they had ignored. And he prayed for the Kingdom and its inhabitants, who now seemed out of place in the world.

And so both oppressor and oppressed were brought before the just and merciful God in prayer that day.

WORSHIP

MAN named Terence, a widower, had had a wife for many years who prayed often and talked constantly of her love for God. And Terence had been sometimes amused and sometimes admiring. And now, these many years after her passing, he wondered what it was that had moved her daily to testify to her love for God.

He asked the Traveler, "What is worship?"

The Traveler replied, "Worship is recognizing that love draws boundaries. It is acknowledging that the great Lover, the one who exists to give love and to be loved, is jealous, as any devoted lover rightfully is. Worship is saying to God, the Lover, 'We belong to each other, you and I, and whatever else I care for, I care for it less than for you.' Hear what The Book says."

The Lord commanded, "You may worship no other god than me. You shall not make yourselves any idols, no images. You must never bow or worship it in any way, for I, the Lord your God, am very possessive. I will not share your affection with any other god!"

Those who trust in idols and call them gods will be disappointed. Those choosing other gods shall all be filled with sorrow. Dear children, keep away from anything that might take God's place in your hearts.

We have come to bring you the Good News that you are invited to turn from the worship of these foolish things and to pray instead to the living God who made heaven and earth and sea and everything in them.

"Understand," the Traveler said, "that idols are more than images of stone or clay. Whatever you bow down to, whatever your heart salutes as its master, that is an idol. All that exists, exists because God, the one Center of the universe, made it. And only that Center merits your full devotion. He alone deserves your songs of gratitude and the daily bending of your hearts toward him."

Terence spoke again. "This God, this Great Being who made all, who gave being to whatever is—can we indeed approach him as if we are speaking to a lover or a friend? Is not One so mighty and so pure too far from us to be approached?"

"One who is truly mighty can stoop down," the Traveler said. "The ruler of a nation bows down to hear the muddled words of his small grandson. And though we know the Lord God is greater than anyone, yet we cannot cower in fear when we are overwhelmed with gratitude." Then the Traveler began to read.

This is the day the Lord has made. We will rejoice and be glad in it.

I bless the holy name of God with all my heart. Yes, I will bless the Lord and not forget the glorious things he does for me. He surrounds me with loving-kindness and tender mercies. He fills my life with good things! My youth is renewed like the eagle's!

Try to realize what this means—the Lord is God! He made us—we are his people, the sheep of his pasture.

Fear God and extol his greatness. Worship him who

made the heaven and the earth, the sea and all its sources.

Come, kneel before the Lord our Maker. Shout with joy before the Lord, O earth! Obey him gladly; come before him, singing with joy.

Go through his open gates with great thanksgiving; enter his courts with praise. Give thanks to him and bless his name. For the Lord is always good. He is always loving and kind, and his faithfulness goes on and on to each succeeding generation.

A woman standing near Terence had a conscience that bore a ponderous load, and she believed she could not draw near to Almighty God, no matter how grateful she might be. She had learned what a burden and an ache it was to commit offenses and not have them forgiven. She asked the Traveler, "Can one who has done what God the Great Being condemns ever bow down to him? Will he not leave us in the dust, wallowing in the refuse of our past?"

The Unknown Traveler warmed at beholding a heart that could feel its unworthiness. He read these words, looking deep into the woman's eyes:

Who may stand before the Lord? Only those with pure hands and hearts, who do not practice dishonesty and lying.

They will receive God's own goodness as their blessing from him, planted in their lives by God himself, their Savior. These are the ones who are allowed to stand before the Lord and worship.

Pray with holy hands lifted up to God, free from sin and anger and resentment.

He could see the birthing of a tear in the woman's eye, for what he had read to her was no consolation.

She did not feel her heart was clean or her hands holy. And he read again.

All day and all night your hand was heavy on me. My sins, too many to count, all caught up with me and I was ashamed to look up. My heart quails within me. My strength evaporated like water on a sunny day until I finally admitted all my sins to you and stopped trying to hide them.

I said to myself, "I will confess them to the Lord." "O Lord," I prayed, "be kind and heal me, for I have confessed my sins." And you forgave me! All my guilt is gone.

He forgives all my sins. He heals me. He ransoms me from hell.

Now I say that each believer should confess his sins to God when he is aware of them, while there is time to be forgiven. Judgment will not touch him if he does.

What happiness for those whose guilt has been forgiven! What joys when sins are covered over! What relief for those who have confessed their sins and God has cleared their record.

Now the repentant woman's one tear had joined with many others. She withdrew from the square, not in anger and not in shame, but in the sad joy that requires time and space by itself, time to linger awhile with God the Forgiver. The woman with the sad joy had not known that mere words could so rain on a dry heart. Yet she was pleased that the God who endowed his creatures with words could so delightfully use them himself.

Terence remembered how his wife had many times walked in the forest near the Valley, sometimes seeming lost in thoughts, sometimes with glad eyes gazing at the ancient pines and the carpet of verdant moss. And he had sometimes followed her, though not so close as to disturb her. And he had heard her singing to the One who gave such joy. Now Terence asked the Traveler, "Our worship of God is a solitary act, is it not?"

The Traveler replied, "Every heart is solitary before the Almighty, for everyone must by himself account for his deeds and misdeeds. How right, how proper it is for everyone to review in his heart throughout the day the good things God has bestowed. Yet how much joy there is in gathering together in a body, proving that there are others who have not forgotten this world's Maker and Redeemer, though it sometimes seems that all the world slights him." Then he read these words:

"Where two or three gather together because they are mine, I will be right there among them," said the Son of God.

Let us not neglect our church meetings, as some people do, but encourage and warn each other, especially now that the day of his coming back again is drawing near.

He made the world and everything in it, and since he is Lord of heaven and earth, he does not live in man-made temples; and human hands cannot minister to his needs—for he has no needs! He himself gives life and breath to everything, and satisfies every need there is.

A man who wore garments carefully chosen was a collector of paintings and sculptures. He prided himself on his love of beauty, and he was pleased whenever the Traveler spoke of how the Creator had formed the great and the small things of the universe and set them together in patterns of delight. He spoke to the Traveler, saying, "Sir, nothing in the world could be more glorious than for people to gather together and sing proper hymns and recite words from The Book with great dignity. How the Creator must

be honored when he beholds the beauty and the measured graciousness of ritual and our holy days. And
how he must savor our raising up stately buildings in
his honor."

The Traveler nodded, yet he did not smile at this.
"This is truth, but it lacks. There is more." Then he
read these words from The Book:

God says, "I hate your show and pretense—your hypoc-
risy of 'honoring' me with your religious feasts and sol-
emn assemblies.

"Away with your hymns of praise—they are mere
noise to my ears. I will not listen to your music, no matter how lovely it is.

"In your holy feasts to God you do not think of me,
but only the food and fellowship and fun.

"Pretty words may hide a wicked heart, just as a pretty glaze covers a common clay pot. These people say they
are mine but do not obey me, and their worship amounts
to mere words learned by rote.

"I want to see a mighty flood of justice—a torrent of
doing good."

God does not live in temples made by human hands.
It is not where we worship that counts, but how we worship—is our worship spiritual and real? Do we have the
Holy Spirit's help? For God is Spirit, and we must have
his help to worship as we should. The Father wants this
kind of worship from us.

Then the Unknown Traveler read these words of
the Son of God so the people would remember that
they could not worship without loving each other:

If you are standing before the altar, offering a sacrifice to
God, and suddenly remember that a friend has something
against you, leave your sacrifice there beside the altar and

*go and apologize and be reconciled to him, and then come
and offer your sacrifice to God.*

"People of the Valley," said the Traveler in a pleading tone, "in this bewildered world, men and women
worship their work, work at their play, and play at
their worship. And this should not be. Your worship
of the Ruler of the universe is not to be theatre. Worship is to pour forth out of you like the language of
love. It is a mingling of praise, adoration, appeals,
sorrow over mistakes, and forgiveness for them, like
the father and child at their finest. And worship is the
embrace that only reconciled lovers can know. When
it occurs, there is nothing like it in this world. It is a
sip from the cup of heaven."

JOY

MADELINE was a woman who had practiced at being sad. Like everyone in the Valley, she had endured sickness, worried over her children, and borne all manner of disappointments. Yet though she had had no more rain nor pain than most, her great delight seemed to be in recounting her lack of delight. Some who knew her pitied her, which is what she wished. Sad people's single happiness is found in being observed in their sadness. But others considered her nothing more than a nurse for her own wounds.

The young ones in the Valley brought sneers to Madeline's downturned mouth. They, she believed, understood little of the hurts of this world, and she knew their laughter arose from a false and trivial view of life. Like most carriers of gloom, she could not imagine that real joy existed. Madeline believed all laughter was only a mask covering a ceaseless scream—at a universe bent on vexing and perplexing its inhabitants. And the more robust the laughter, she thought, the more pitiful the internal wailing.

Martin, who had been the first of the People of the Valley to meet the Unknown Traveler, knew Madeline. He perceived how she saw life through a cruel lens, knew that to see things as she saw them was to waste one's eyes. Yet on the days when bad had clearly triumphed over good in his life, he understood her, and why her heart had wrapped dark bandages around itself.

Martin said to the Traveler, "What cause is there to be happy in this world?" And he asked this not with the tone of a young scholar striving to look grave, but with the tone of a man asking a question men should ask.

Then the Traveler replied, "Have you not felt a baby's soft cheek against your own? Have you not known the wave that washes through you when your wife's lips touch your tired neck? Have you not cried those peculiar, exquisite tears when you walked in a misty meadow at sunset and felt that the larks' song and the violets' blossoms had been put there for your liking? Have you not lain in your warm bed on a snowy night and remembered the evening's banquet, with food and drink to spare?

"Have you not heard a man awkward in love suddenly dripping poetry from his mouth because a woman's embrace had fired his soul? Have you not heard a singer pouring out a rhapsody that seemed to trickle down from heaven? Have you not passed through your doorway and been greeted by the smell of fresh-baked bread? Have you never marveled at a falcon hovering over a summer field? Have you never stood at a window with your hands on your children's shoulders, watching the waters of March trickling across the stones of the street?"

And Martin said, "We have all known these things, and more besides. Yet sometimes we pause in the midst of laughter, in the midst of loving, in the midst of bouncing a giggling child on our knees. We pause, and for a moment the sweetness slackens, and we wonder why it is we take joy in these things."

"And have you ever," asked the Traveler, "questioned the joy you felt in God, Almighty God?" Then he picked up The Book and read these words:

Rejoice before the Lord your God in everything you do.

The joy of the Lord is your strength. You must not be dejected and sad!

Serve the Lord with reverent fear; rejoice with trembling.

Then the Traveler paused, and seeing anticipation in Martin's face, he continued with these words of one who loved God:

Lord, the gladness you have given us is far greater than the joys at harvest time as we gaze at the bountiful crops.

I will be glad, yes, filled with joy because of you. I will sing your praises, O Lord God above all gods.

God's laws are perfect. They protect us, make us wise, and give us joy and light.

Your words are what sustain me; they are food to my hungry soul. They bring joy to my sorrowing heart and delight me. How proud I am to bear your name, O Lord.

There is a river of joy flowing through the City of our God—the sacred home of the God above all gods.

"Does it seem so strange to you, dear friends, to sing of joy in God? Through ages and ages men make rhymes and sing songs about the sweetness of love, the comforts of hearth and home, the beauties of trees and flowers, the glories of victory in battle. And this is right. Yet how the soul is stirred by the joy of God! No song ever sung for lover or homeland compares with the anthems that have come from the minds of those animated by holy joy. You have heard the sweetest anthems ever sung poured forth from

143

those whose hearts were spent. They sang, despaired, and almost died. Then they clutched God, and sang an even sweeter song." And when the Traveler had said this, he began to read again.

Make everyone rejoice who puts his trust in you. Keep them shouting for joy because you are defending them. Fill all who love you with your happiness.

I will always trust in you and in your mercy and shall rejoice in your salvation.

You feed us with blessings from your own table and let us drink from your rivers of delight.

I lie awake at night thinking of you, of how much you have helped me—and how I rejoice through the night beneath the protecting shadow of your wings.

Happy are all who search for God, and always do his will. Your laws are my joyous treasure forever.

Shout, O earth! Break forth into song, O mountains and forests, yes, and every tree! For the Lord is glorified!

When the Traveler spoke these words, he lifted his eyes from the pages, and his face shone with elation.

Madeline's cloud, invisible, yet thicker than the gray clouds of autumn that hung over the Valley that day, had not dispersed. But she had been touched by what Martin said to the Traveler. Martin, it seemed, was a perplexed inquirer, unsure that all the questions of his youth had been answered. And Madeline was past asking questions, for she had pronounced the universe ugly and hostile.

But even those who are decided and fixed can sometimes raise questions. And that is what Madeline did on that day.

"Sir, is it possible that our joy in this world is diminished by our yearning for something greater?" And to assure the Traveler that what she asked was not merely selfish and childish, she continued, "I mean to say, were we created for something else than this world, beautiful though it is? We love to look upon beauty, but something—or someone—calls us not to observe, but to unite. We want not only to see, but to live with, and live in, and be lost in. And this eludes us."

Those standing near Madeline stared in disbelief, for they had never heard her speak well of anything. They had known for years that even when the cherry trees in the Valley burst forth in pink vestments, Madeline's countenance was not altered. But Martin understood her, for he knew that underneath the bitterness was someone who dreamed of noble and enduring things.

The Traveler understood her also. And he read these words:

The time will come when God's redeemed will all come home again. They shall come with singing, filled with joy and everlasting gladness; sorrow and mourning will all disappear. The wilderness and desert will rejoice in those days. The desert will blossom with flowers. There will be an abundance of flowers and singing and joy! The mountains and hills, the trees of the field—all the world around you—will rejoice.

Rejoice greatly, O my people! Shout with joy! For look—your King is coming!

Then he paused and said, "I have more to say to you of what is to come—what lies beyond this world, and what awaits you." And so that he would not leave them merely perplexed, he read them this command, one of the sublimest ever written, one most joyous to execute:

Talk with each other much about the Lord, quoting psalms and hymns and singing sacred songs, making music in your hearts to the Lord!

And even those who scoffed at the notion of God were pleased to hear that God commanded music of his beloved ones.

THE FUTURE

MARTIN had an old
uncle who lived on an immense estate in the Valley.
He was a hardened, bitter man, a man whose legacy
in the world was a massive fortune of wealth—and a
vast desert of feeling. This old man cared little for
anyone. Every person on this earth suffers, at certain
seasons, from an eclipse of the heart, but Martin's old
uncle had chosen to lodge perpetually in the darkness.

Members of his family had tried for years to break
through the hard husk he had formed around himself.
Martin hoped that some change might occur before
the old man faced the prospect of dying.

On this day the old uncle was there, though he
gave little credence to the Unknown Traveler and to
The Book from which he had read. But he did listen
as an arrogant young man stepped forward and spoke
with an abrasive tone to the Traveler.

"Sir, you have spoken to us time and time again
about this loving Father who creates us and rescues
us. How could one so full of love allow his beloved
creatures to perish? These silly rumors of punishment
are not to be taken seriously, are they? Are they not
mere fabrications of parents trying to invoke fear in
unruly children?"

The Traveler looked around the square, perceiving

that even some gray-haired grandparents were still, in some ways, unruly children. And he knew that so many People of the Valley lived in the realm of wishful thinking, unwilling to face the painful truths of existence. He read them these words from The Book, knowing that some would laugh, for men may whistle in graveyards and laugh at a vision of judgment:

Those who forget God have no hope.

They are like rushes without any mire to grow in, or grass without water to keep it alive. Suddenly it begins to wither, even before it is cut.

A man without God is trusting in a spider's web. Everything he counts on will collapse. If he counts on his home for security, it will not last.

At dawn he seems so strong and virile, like a green plant. His branches spread across the garden. His roots are in the stream, down among the stones.

But when he disappears, he is not even missed! That is all he can look forward to! And others spring up from the earth to replace him!

Martin's old uncle shifted his weight onto his heels as he listened. He liked the words of the arrogant youth who had spoken. But there was a stinging truth in the words of the Traveler.

"All lovers must come to dust. All of you are lovers of something or someone—yourselves, or what you used to be, or your possessions, or the dream of having possessions. What becomes of the thing you love is what will become of you. That is why The Book tells you, line after line, to love the One Being that made all things—for love will not come to dust."

God is both kind and severe. He is very hard on those who disobey, but very good to you if you continue to love and trust him. But if you do not, you too will be cut off.

Sir, you have spoken to us
          time and time again
     about this loving Father
        who creates us and rescues us.
How could one so full of love
     allow his beloved creatures
               to perish?

Do you not realize that you can choose your own master? You can choose sin—with death—or else obedience—with acquittal. The one to whom you offer yourself—he will take you and be your master and you will be his slave.

The Lord's face is hard against those who do evil. Those who live immoral lives, who are idol worshipers, adulterers, or homosexuals will have no share in his Kingdom. Neither will thieves or greedy people, drunkards, slanderers, or robbers.

You can be sure of this: The Kingdom of Christ and of God will never belong to anyone who is impure or greedy, for a greedy person is really an idol worshiper—he loves and worships the good things of this life more than God.

Do not be fooled by those who try to excuse these sins, for the terrible wrath of God is upon all those who do them. For the truth about God is known to them instinctively. God has put this knowledge in their hearts. Since earliest times men have seen the earth and sky and all God made, and have known of his existence and great eternal power. So they will have no excuse when they stand before God at Judgment Day.

Those who do not trust Christ have already been tried and condemned for not believing in the only Son of God. Their sentence is based on this fact: that the Light from heaven came into the world, but they loved the darkness more than the Light, for their deeds were evil.

They hated the heavenly Light because they wanted to sin in the darkness. They stayed away from that Light for fear their sins would be exposed and they would be punished.

There is going to come a day of wrath when God will be the just Judge of all the world. He will give each one whatever his deeds deserve. He will terribly punish those who fight against the truth of God and walk in evil

*ways—God's anger will be poured out upon them. The
wicked shall be sent away to hell.*

Martin's old uncle noticed that as the Traveler
continued speaking, the arrogant young man withdrew from the square and went to his home. The old
man wanted to do the same, but he could not move.
Though his heart was old, there was still hope within
it, and he waited, wanting the Traveler to speak
words of comfort and hope to those who had wasted
the years God had given them. But before the comfort came the harder edge of the truth.

"Do you think," the Traveler asked, "that God
wishes to scare you into loving him and giving yourselves to him? No, indeed. The holy risk that God
has taken is this: He made you all, knowing you could
love him—or reject him. Love given unwillingly is
not love. You cannot be yanked into God's Kingdom,
yet you can be coaxed by his love. And I would do you
wrong not to tell you of the consequences of not loving the Lover.

"What is hell? You see images of flame and an abyss
and horrid smells. All are true, for these are pictures
of anyone who says, 'I am my own.' You have all
known people who already seemed to be in hell,
smoldering in their self-interest. With no joy do I
speak about these things, yet I must. I do not lie, The
Book does not lie. Those who spend this life co-
cooned in themselves will surely enter the next life in
the same way. Can you bear to think of this—no
tomorrows, no plans, no rest, no possibilities? Only a
loveless forever and forever without end."

You were lost, without God, without hope.
*But God loved the world so much that he gave his only
Son so that anyone who believes in him shall not perish*

but have eternal life. God did not send his Son into the world to condemn it, but to save it. Those who believe and are baptized will be saved.

Now your sins are washed away, and you are set apart for God, and he has accepted you because of what the Lord Jesus Christ and the Spirit of our God have done for you. Though once your heart was full of darkness, now it is full of light from the Lord.

Now we rejoice in our wonderful new relationship with God—all because of what our Lord Jesus Christ has done in dying for our sins—making us friends of God.

Death came into the world because of what one man—Adam—did, and it is because of what this other man—Christ—has done that now there is the resurrection from the dead.

Everyone dies because all of us are related to Adam, being members of his sinful race, and wherever there is sin, death results. But all who are related to Christ will rise again.

One old man, a man who had once been a close companion of Martin's uncle, was warmed when he heard these words. He had lived a life of kindness and compassion. Though he was loved by all who knew him, he was worn out from living. As he felt his feeble heart drumming faintly within him, he longed to hear what life would be like after this one had passed away.

"Traveler," he said, his voice hardly more than a whisper, "tell us what we will be like in the next world."

The Traveler began to speak again.

When this tent we live in now is taken down—when we die and leave these bodies—we will have wonderful new bodies in heaven, homes that will be ours forevermore.

How weary we grow of our present bodies. That is

why we look forward eagerly to the day when we shall have heavenly bodies which we shall put on like new clothes.

These earthly bodies make us groan and sigh, but we would not like to think of dying and having no bodies at all. We want to slip into our new bodies so that these dying bodies will be swallowed up by everlasting life. This is what God has prepared for us.

We look forward with confidence to our heavenly bodies, realizing that every moment we spend in these earthly bodies is time spent away from our eternal home in heaven with Jesus. And we are not afraid, but are quite content to die, for then we will be at home with the Lord.

This world is not our home; we are looking forward to our everlasting home in heaven.

I pray that your hearts will be flooded with light so that you can see something of the future he has called you to share. And you are looking forward to the joys of heaven, and have been ever since the Gospel first was preached to you.

Martin had been observing his uncle's face, and he could see that the Traveler's words were moving the old man. He was not surprised when the old man spoke up.

"How can we be certain? I have lived more than eighty years, and I have seen good men and bad men buried. Do we have any assurance that the good will endure?"

The Traveler said, "What assurance can I give you? I cannot write out a guarantee for you. If you cannot believe that the Son of God was raised up from death, you will not believe that anyone else will be raised up. But in a universe where an executed carpenter can rise from the dead, anything is possible. Listen closely to the testimony of one who believed."

153

You will not leave me among the dead; you will not allow your beloved one to rot in the grave. You have let me experience the joys of life and the exquisite pleasures of your own eternal presence.

Your goodness and unfailing kindness shall be with me all of my life, and afterwards I will live with you forever in your home.

God has reserved for his children the priceless gift of eternal life.

"And listen now to another man, assured in his heart that the God who sent his Son to die for us would not let us be lost."

Victory is ours through Christ who loved us enough to die for us. For I am convinced that nothing can ever separate us from his love.

Death cannot, and life cannot. The angels will not, and all the powers of hell itself cannot keep God's love away. Nothing will ever be able to separate us from the love of God demonstrated by our Lord Jesus Christ when he died for us.

The end will come when he will turn the Kingdom over to God the Father, having put down all enemies of every kind. For Christ will be King until he has defeated all his enemies, including the last enemy—death. This too must be defeated and ended.

Martin's uncle spoke again. "What did the Son of God himself say? Did he leave any words of assurance?"

The Traveler nodded and began to read.

I give them eternal life and they shall never perish. No one shall snatch them away from me, for my Father has given them to me, and he is more powerful than anyone

154

else, so no one can kidnap them from me. I and the Father are one.

The old uncle spoke again. "Traveler, when I was a child I heard stories about heaven. Long ago I dismissed them, every one, believing they were mere tales told to amuse or to bewilder. Somehow, now—I cannot explain it—I am so weary of this world, yet not certain that the next will be better. I pray it is more than a replica of this one."

The Traveler replied, "In the eyes of this world you have done well. Many who envy your position would wish to continue such an existence through all eternity. Yet you would not?" The Traveler was being kind and cruel, with kindness at the fore.

Stung by his words, but not angry, the old man said, "Is there in The Book a picture of heaven, an image we can fix our minds on?"

"Are you longing to hear stories from your childhood again?" the Traveler asked. "What can it mean to you, hearing airy fantasies now, you who have succeeded by this world's standards? Are you not an adult?"

The old man sighed, not mindful now of the fear of appearing undignified. "I am an old man, tired, pacing on from one day to the next like a gathering of ashes that have almost cooled. Nothing matters now except the Truth. Nothing matters to one with his foot slipping on the edge of eternity, nothing except what endures."

As the Traveler began to read again, Martin moved through the crowd to stand at his uncle's side.

The time will come when all the earth is filled, as the waters fill the sea, with an awareness of the glory of the Lord. Your eyes will see the King in his beauty, and the highlands of heaven far away.

155

I, John, saw the Holy City, the new Jerusalem, coming down from God out of heaven. It was a glorious sight, beautiful as a bride at her wedding.

I heard a loud shout from the throne saying, "Look, the home of God is now among men, and he will live with them and they will be his people; yes, God himself will be among them. He will wipe away all tears from their eyes, and there shall be no more death, nor sorrow, nor crying, nor pain. All of that has gone forever."

The city itself was pure, transparent gold like glass! The wall was made of jasper, and was built on twelve layers of foundation stones inlaid with gems. The twelve gates were made of pearls—each gate from a single pearl! And the main street was pure, transparent gold, like glass.

Some of the listeners laughed to themselves, for they dismissed it all as tales told by dreamers who had failed in this world. But not all laughed. Some, though they knew the Valley had its beauties, were dazzled by these pictures of something more beautiful. Then the Traveler continued to read.

No temple could be seen in the city, for the Lord God Almighty and the Lamb are worshiped in it everywhere. And the city has no need of sun or moon to light it, for the glory of God and of the Lamb illuminate it. Its light will light the nations of the earth, and the rulers of the world will come and bring their glory to it.

There shall be nothing in the city which is evil; for the throne of God and of the Lamb will be there, and his servants will worship him. And they shall see his face; and his name shall be written on their foreheads.

And there will be no night there—no need for lamps or sun—for the Lord God will be their light; and they shall reign forever and ever.

156

Martin had never seen his uncle shed a single tear, and as he looked now at his craggy face, so seared and worn, he wondered if those dry gray eyes could ever bring forth tears. Yet one trickled in a meandering way down his leathery cheek. Martin was not sure what the tear was for—perhaps for remorse, perhaps for a remembrance of a sunnier day years ago when tales of heaven could be easily believed, perhaps for joy at believing now that the tales were more than tales. Martin lightly touched his uncle's arm. The old man turned to him, his lips moving slightly as though a thought had not yet formed itself into words.

The Unknown Traveler looked intently at Martin and his uncle. Then he stared for a moment at a page in the open Book, finally closing it. His eyes met those of a small boy, and though no word was spoken, the child knew what the Traveler wanted. He stepped forward and held out his arms, and the Traveler gently placed The Book in them. He placed a hand on the child's head and looked into his wide, quizzical eyes. "Little one, remember this: The Book must not go unread. Tell that to your father and your mother, and when you are a man, remember it, and teach it to your children and to their children." Then he addressed the People of the Valley for the last time.

"People of the Valley, I will leave this place in the morning. Go to your homes. It is late in the day. Remember to remember. Do not forget that I came here, but if you do, at least do not forget The Book. It is yours, as it belongs to everyone in every place." Then the Traveler spoke these words from The Book.

Since we have a Kingdom nothing can destroy, let us please God by serving him with thankful hearts, and with holy fear and awe.

The People of the Valley began to make their quiet way homeward. No one was left in the square except Martin and his uncle and the Traveler. Suddenly a nighthawk shuttled by in its angular flight and signaled to all that it was dusk.

The Traveler said, "Martin, I will abide under your roof tonight and will leave early."

Martin nodded, then turned his gaze on the old man, who in turn looked at the Traveler. The Traveler smiled slightly, and the old man, whose face still showed the track where the tear had traversed down, turned to Martin and spoke in a whisper. "Such a day, nephew. I have so much I wish to talk about with you."

Then Traveler placed his hand on the old man's shoulder and said in a voice not much louder than the breeze, "Remember these words of the Son of God."

Come to me and I will give you rest. I am gentle and humble, and you shall find rest for your souls, for I give you only light burdens.

THE TRAVELER
DEPARTS
THE VALLEY

HEN morning broke, spilling its rose and lavender haze over the sleeping Valley, the Unknown Traveler walked to the hill on which he had had his first view of the Valley. He shivered a bit in the morning cool and gathered his coat around him. As he stood looking down on the rooftops of the Valley, he saw a lone figure running toward him, waving anxiously. It was Martin.

"Wait, Traveler! You mustn't leave without giving us all a good farewell!"

The Traveler smiled. Martin's face was flushed. It was clear that he had run all the way from his house.

"Ah, Martin, you did not need to disturb your sleep on my account. I told you last night that I would leave quietly."

"We owe you so much. I do hate to have you leave us."

The Traveler stretched out his hand and gripped Martin's shoulder, which was shivering under his dressing gown. "Friend, you owe me nothing. Whatever is of value in this bent world is owing to Almighty God. If you honor anyone, honor him. You need not even remember me. Only remember that great treasure you have, The Book. Nothing would please me more than that."

"May I walk with you a while?"

"You are hardly dressed, Martin. It is a chilly

dawn, and I must be going. I have people to see. There is so much to be done."

Martin looked into the incorruptible brown eyes of the Traveler. "Yes—yes, I am sure you do. There are so many others who don't know—or who have forgotten—the Truth." Then Martin did something that surprised himself: He extended his arms and embraced the Traveler. And the Traveler held him tightly before speaking again.

"Go home, Martin," the Unknown Traveler said in a mild voice. "Go home, and warm yourself, and live in love, and cling to the Truth like a burr clinging to your sleeve in summer. Cling to it, live for it, share it, die in it, rest in it." And with those words the Traveler released Martin and hastened down the hill, hardly leaving tracks on the silvery mantle of frost.

Martin turned and ran back to the Valley, his eyes fixed on the smoke curling from the chimney that he knew was his. He could not remember when his senses had been so roused by the sight and sound and texture of morning. And as his feet skimmed over frosted pebbles, he was glad he could watch a day be born.

At the foot of the hill the Traveler turned, glad to see that Martin had gone home. He paused for a moment, leaning against his walking stick. Thinking of the People of the Valley, he wished for a moment that he might say to each of them these words he knew from The Book:

My dear brothers, since future victory is sure, be strong and steady, always abounding in the Lord's work.

And while he paused he prayed that the People of the Valley might awaken every morning and sing the song written in The Book:

Holy, holy, holy is the Lord Almighty. The whole earth is filled with his glory.

God's Man is here! Bless him, Lord! Praise God in highest heaven!

A NOTE
TO THE
READER

When the Unknown Traveler is reciting the words of "The Book," he is, of course, quoting the words of the Bible. The version used here is *The Book*—that is, *The Living Bible*, the popular paraphrase of the Bible by Kenneth N. Taylor.

The author of *Secrets from The Book* chose to weave together Bible passages that relate to the subjects in each chapter. People who are not familiar with the Bible—and many who are familiar with it—often find it puzzling to read, since its teachings on specific subjects are widely separated across its many pages. One of the purposes of *Secrets from The Book* is to help organize the Bible's teachings on the topics most crucial for living the spiritual life. In organizing these passages and in writing the story of the Unknown Traveler and the People of the Valley, the author chose to focus not so much on theological doctrines as on ethical teachings. The "secrets" are not theological mysteries but, rather, guidelines for living.

However, references to the particular chapters and verses in the Bible were not included. It was felt that including these references in the text would interrupt the flow of the words. Some readers may wish to locate the passages in the Bible. For help in doing this, Bible references—chapters and verses—are listed here by the page numbers in which they are quoted in this book.

THE PEOPLE OF THE VALLEY
Page 16: Hebrews 1:1-3

FINDING THE BOOK
Page 21: Ecclesiastes 1:2, 8; 2:11
Page 22: Proverbs 8:1-4, 10, 22-26, 33-36
Page 22: Proverbs 9:10
Page 24: John 10:10; 7:37-38; 8:32

WORSHIP

Pages 133-134: Exodus 20:3-5; Isaiah 42:17; Psalm 16:4; 1 John 5:21;
    Acts 14:15
Pages 134-135: Psalms 118:24; 103:1-2, 4-5; 100:3; Revelation 14:7;
    Psalms 95:6; 100:1-2, 4-5
Page 135: Psalm 24:3-6; 1 Timothy 2:8
Page 136: Psalms 32:4; 40:12; 32:5; 41:4; 103:3-4; 32:6; 32:1-2
Page 137: Matthew 18:20; Hebrews 10:25; Acts 17:24-25
Page 138: Amos 5:21-23; Zechariah 7:6; Proverbs 26:23; Isaiah 29:13;
    Amos 5:24; Acts 7:48-49; John 4:23-24
Pages 138-139: Matthew 5:24

JOY

Page 143: Deuteronomy 12:18; Nehemiah 8:10; Psalm 2:11
Page 143: Psalms 4:7; 9:2; 19:7-8; Jeremiah 15:16; Psalm 46:4
Page 144: Psalms 5:11; 13:5; 36:8; 63:6-7; 119:1-3; Isaiah 44:23
Page 145: Isaiah 51:11; 55:12; 35:1-2; Zechariah 9:9
Page 146: Ephesians 5:19

THE FUTURE

Page 148: Job 8:11-19
Pages 148-151: Romans 11:22; 6:16; 1 Peter 3:12; 1 Corinthians 6:9-10;
    Ephesians 5:5-6; Romans 1:19-20; John 3:18-20; Romans 2:5-6, 8;
    Psalm 9:17
Pages 151-152: Ephesians 2:12; John 3:16-17; Mark 16:16;
    1 Corinthians 6:11; Ephesians 5:8; Romans 5:11; 6:4;
    1 Corinthians 15:21-22
Pages 152-153: 2 Corinthians 5:1-2, 4-6; Hebrews 13:14;
    Ephesians 1:18; Colossians 1:5
Page 154: Psalms 16:10-11; 23:6; 1 Peter 1:4
Page 154: Romans 8:37-39; 1 Corinthians 15:24-26
Pages 154-155: John 10:28-30
Pages 155-156: Habakkuk 2:14; Isaiah 33:17; Revelation 21:2-4, 18-21
Page 156: Revelation 21:22-24; 22:3-5
Page 157: Hebrews 12:28
Page 158: Matthew 11:28-30

THE TRAVELER DEPARTS THE VALLEY

Page 160: 1 Corinthians 15:58
Page 161: Isaiah 6:3; Matthew 21:9

ABOUT THE AUTHOR

J. Stephen Lang has published his devotional prose and poetry in numerous Christian periodicals, including *Moody Monthly, Eternity, The War Cry, Discipleship Journal, Christian History, Home Life, Liguorian,* and *The Upper Room.* His poetry has appeared in such literary journals as *Poem, The Lyric, Plains Poetry Journal, Muse,* and *Roanoke Review.*

In his best-selling *Complete Book of Bible Trivia* (Tyndale House, 1988), he focused on the lighter aspects of the Bible, its many fascinating details of character and incident. In this book he shifts the focus to the more serious, life-affecting aspects of biblical truth, the great themes rather than the small details. Commenting on the difference in the two books, the author stated, "The first book was intended to be a book of facts. This is intended to be a book of insight."

He holds the B.A. in Bible and theology (Scarritt College) and the M.A. in communications (Wheaton College). He is an editor with Tyndale House Publishers in Wheaton, Illinois.